Praise for *How to Own the World Before You're 30*

"Andrew Craig's investment philosophy changed my financial life when I first read the original How to Own the World years ago. This new book delivers the same powerful lessons with fresh relevance for under-thirties navigating today's world. Andrew's ability to communicate finance topics in a way anyone can understand is second to none. But for me, in a time that can often feel overwhelmingly negative, his greatest talent is making you feel genuinely optimistic about your financial future."

Damien Jordan, leading UK personal finance YouTuber, podcaster and blogger

"It's almost unfashionable these days to make the case for money, capital markets and wealth creation – but this book does exactly that, and does it brilliantly.

Craig shows a younger audience that getting rich isn't inevitable, but it is absolutely possible if you're willing to do the work and follow some simple principles. Most importantly, he makes it clear why it's worth trying – something too many people seem to have given up on nowadays."

Rob Dix, author of Seven Myths about Money *and* The Price of Money

"The mark of a civilized person is understanding society's various technologies. Money is possibly the most fantastic invention since bread and the wheel. Money is a technology that communities use to trade debts across space and time. Debts such as what your younger self owes your future self. Take the time to understand money. As I said about the prequel to this book: 'If you want just one book on investment from the cacophony, you couldn't do much better.'"

Professor Michael Mainelli, Lord Mayor of London 2023–4, Chairman, Z/Yen Group, and President, London Chamber of Commerce & Industry

"Andrew Craig has made it his mission not only to put the mysterious world of personal finance in plain, comprehensible English, but to help people find ways to beat the global money-printing contagion with which we are blighted. Good for him. Highly readable and highly rated."

Dominic Frisby, journalist and author of The Secret History of Gold, Bitcoin: The Future of Money?, Life after the State and Daylight Robbery

"Finance doesn't have to be boring, complicated nonsense. The original version of How to Own the World broke it all down in plain English, showing you how investing actually works, and why you should do it. This new version, aimed at under-thirties, gives you all the tools you need to make a big difference to your future. Inspiring and super accessible. Definitely a must-read."

Ian Peacock, fintech CEO and Sloan Fellow, London Business School

How to Own the World Before You're 30

How to Own the World Before You're 30

A Plain English Guide to Investing Globally and Making Money

ANDREW CRAIG

JOHN MURRAY BUSINESS

First published by John Murray Business in 2025
An imprint of John Murray Press

1

A CIP catalogue record for this title is available from the British Library.

Trade Paperback ISBN 9781399800235
ebook ISBN 9781399800259

Typeset by KnowledgeWorks Global Ltd.

Printed and bound in Great Britain by Clays Ltd, Elcograf S.p.A.

John Murray Press policy is to use papers that are natural, renewable and recyclable products and made from wood grown in sustainable forests. The logging and manufacturing processes are expected to conform to the environmental regulations of the country of origin.

John Murray Press
Carmelite House
50 Victoria Embankment
London EC4Y 0DZ

John Murray Business
Hachette Book Group
123 South Broad Street
Ste 2750
Philadelphia, PA 19109, USA

www.johnmurraybusiness.com

John Murray Press, part of Hodder & Stoughton Limited
An Hachette UK company

The authorized representative in the EEA is Hachette Ireland, 8 Castlecourt Centre, Dublin 15, D15 XTP3, Ireland (email: info@hbgi.ie)

This book is dedicated to my wife, Rachel Anne Craig.
For enduring the mood swings and madness with
such grace, and for being quite the most eagle-eyed,
detail-oriented and diligent proofreader on earth.
I truly couldn't have written any of *our* books
without you.

Contents

About the author

Andrew Craig is a best-selling finance author, entrepreneur and the founder of the personal finance website www.plainenglishfinance.co.uk, which was established in 2011.

His stated mission with the company is 'to improve the financial affairs of as many people as possible'.

He believes that you owe it to yourself to learn about money and investment because doing so is life-changing.

Since launching Plain English Finance, Andrew has been featured in numerous British national and specialist financial publications, including *The Telegraph*, *The Financial Times*, *The Mail on Sunday*, *CityAM*, *The Mirror*, *The Spectator*, *Shares*, *Investors' Chronicle* and *MoneyWeek*.

Andrew's first book, *How to Own the World*, has been one of the top-selling personal finance titles in the UK for several years, earning thousands of positive reviews on Amazon, Audible and Goodreads.

His latest book, *Our Future is Biotech* (published in August 2024), reflects his enthusiasm for the transformative potential of the biotechnology industry.

Andrew began his finance career in the late 1990s on the Eurobond desk at SBC Warburg (now UBS) before transitioning to equities, where he joined the smaller companies team. From 2015 to 2021, he was a partner at WG Partners LLP, a specialist life sciences and biotech investment bank. Throughout his career, Andrew has met with senior management teams from over 1,000 companies and engaged with hundreds of professional investors.

Andrew lives in Hampshire, England, with his wife, Rachel, and their two young children, Ella and Oscar.

A note on the present edition

Ever since the first edition of *How to Own the World* was published as long ago as 2012, people have been getting in touch with me and my team to ask about the possibility of a version of the book for a younger audience.

We have had parents, grandparents, uncles, aunts, great-uncles and great-aunts suggest that they would love to have a book to give their children, grandchildren, nieces and nephews.

We've also had a good number of schoolteachers and university lecturers suggest that they would welcome a book for their respective audiences.

Given this feedback, as a team, we initially explored the idea of a book aimed at teenagers some years ago. Happily, our publisher was sufficiently taken with the idea to offer us a book deal, and we set about the task of wrestling the original adult version of the book into a format which would work for a younger audience.

Fast-forward a year or three, and the project evolved somewhat. Cards on the table, I was finding it quite hard to write a book that would work for teenagers. Much as I pride myself on the "plain English" nature of everything I seek to do, I found it hard to write in a voice that could appeal to that audience. I suppose I'm just a bit too long in the tooth by now!

We also felt that a book for under-thirties would be of more practical use than one aimed at teenagers. With the best will in the world, even if I did the best possible job with a book for teenagers, few would be likely to be able to take the proactive steps required to make a real difference to their financial future. A book aimed at twenty-some-things was more likely to have the tangible impact we wanted it to have.

Along the way, we made one other decision: to seek to make the book relevant to a much larger audience globally. The original version of *How to Own the World* is very focused on the British market. I wanted this new version to focus on many of the most fundamental, evergreen truths of personal finance wherever you're based in the world.

I've also been able to fold in what I view as some of my 'greatest hits' content from all three of my existing books. This version incorporates the crucial and elegant idea of '100 minus your age' from my second book, *Live on Less, Invest the Rest*, for example. It also has sections on the impact of negative press bias on how people think about finance, and on how we might strive to be rather more positive about the world, and about capitalism more generally. Many of these ideas featured in my third book, *Our Future is Biotech*.

As such, what I hope I have produced here is a book that can and should be hugely helpful for the financial future and prospects of as wide an audience as possible – from smart teenagers all the way up to people in their late twenties and beyond who may already be some way into their career – and almost no matter where such people might be based in the world.

I hope that I have been successful in that endeavour and that you, the reader, will get a huge amount out of the book wherever you are – and even if you might be a little older than 30!

Very best wishes,
Andrew Craig, August 2025

Introduction

Not everyone wants to be rich. Nowadays it can actually be quite fashionable to say that you don't, but *many* people do. And as we are going to see in this book – everyone should. Everyone really, really should.

Money is sometimes described as 'the root of all evil'. This is arguably one of the silliest and most unhelpful ideas of all time. Ultimately, money is just a technology. In fact it is arguably *the* most important technology we have ever invented as a species, at least as far as human progress, health and happiness are concerned.

Without the invention of money and the various capital markets that followed – which we are going to trot through in this book – we wouldn't be able to enjoy nearly all of the wonderful things we mostly take for granted nowadays, from food and shelter, running water and flushing toilets, all the way through to foreign travel, the internet, smart phones, flat screen TVs, fashion, films, music and gaming.

To understand this point about money being nothing more than a technology, we need to go back in time a few thousand years to understand why it was invented. As we shall see, all of us are incredibly lucky that it was.

In early human societies, the economy, such as it was, was based on a barter system. That is to say that someone with food, for example, might want to swap some of that food for clothing or a tool or weapon.

This system enabled early human societies to improve their productivity, become slightly richer and make life a little bit better overall for everyone, because people were able to *specialize*. One group of people, such as farmers, could spend their days focused on food production, and others, such as weavers or blacksmiths, on the production of things like clothing or tools.

Bartering was better than each person or family trying to do everything themselves. That said, it still wasn't ideal. A farmer who wanted new clothes or shoes for his family would have to find someone who had those things available and who, at that precise moment in time, wanted what the farmer had just produced. This was tricky when you consider that most of the farmer's products were perishable and seasonal, and very difficult to store and transport too.

As a result, several thousand years ago somebody very smart came up with the idea of using something as a *medium of exchange* and a *store of value* – what we now refer to as 'money'.

At a very basic level, the invention of money just simplified how people were able to swap things: a farmer could swap a cow or a chicken for some *money*, and then swap that money days, weeks, months or even years later, for whatever else he or she might want, such as a shirt or a pair of shoes. If he or she sold enough cows or chickens over time, he or she would eventually be able to swap all that saved-up money for something much bigger – like a horse, boat, or even a home.

The development of money was absolutely critical to the development of everything else. Over thousands of years, human beings used all sorts of things as money, including seashells, feathers, rocks, tea, beads and even squirrel pelts. In Roman times, soldiers were often 'paid' in salt – or 'sal' in Latin, which is where the word 'salary' comes from.

For what it is worth, over time, our ancestors came to realize that precious metals were probably the best raw material to use as money. Gold and silver have certain qualities that make them particularly suited to being used as money. We'll look at these in more detail later in the book when we cover some of the key financial products you will want to understand to increase your chances of becoming wealthy.

For now, it is enough to stress that far from being 'the root of all evil', money has been one of the most important tools for lifting us out of a life that used to be 'solitary, poor, nasty, brutish, and short'[1] for most people.

---

[1] This is a famous quote from a 17th-century British philosopher named Thomas Hobbes, from his book *Leviathan*.

All too few of us today realize just how awful life was for most human beings ever born throughout history. Not that long ago, nearly everyone was extremely poor and life was very hard indeed. It is estimated that, in 1820, roughly 90% of the world's population lived in extreme poverty. Today that number is around 10%. In 1800, nearly 90% of people in the world could not read or write. Today more than 85% of our species can, which is great news for so many reasons. In 1800, more than 40% of children died before they reached their fifth birthday. Today, only around 4% do, and that number is significantly lower in the rich, developed world and constantly improving in most of the developing world as well.

The amazing progress we have made in the last few hundred years, which has improved the lives of many billions of us enormously, has come largely as a result of the invention of money and, in the last two centuries in particular, the invention of various financial markets based on money, such as the stock market.[2]

Perhaps a far better idea than 'money is the root of all evil' is the other famous saying: 'Money makes the world go round'!

By the end of this book, you will understand enough about such things to make use of them and very significantly increase the chance that you become wealthy as a result.

Of course, being wealthy increases the chance that you can really enjoy life, and have the freedom to do things like travel, or really invest in the things (and people) that you love.

Perhaps even more important, however, if you care about things like the environment, poverty, hunger, or violence in the developing world, and you want to do something about those things, you'll be able to do far more if you take care of your money first, and a great deal more if you become wealthy.

There is a famous quote, often attributed to one of the Founding Fathers of the US, Benjamin Franklin, which summarizes this idea quite nicely:

> To do good, you must first do well.

---

[2] A very good book on this whole subject is *Money: A Story of Humanity* by David McWilliams.

Or, put another way: 'You can't pour from an empty cup'. The wealthier you are, the more you can do, both in terms of fun and perhaps slightly selfish stuff, like taking that dream holiday or owning your dream car, but also in terms of making a contribution to the state of the world.

The next key point to make about all of this is that understanding money is the number one factor in whether you will become wealthy or not. The reason so many people struggle financially is because they never learnt enough about money or financial markets. In fact, the significant majority of people learn almost nothing at all about money, even today, many centuries after it was invented.

To some extent, this might seem like a statement of the glaringly obvious. If you don't understand money, you're unlikely to become rich. Duh!

But I would argue that, although many of us get the idea that very few people understand money and finance properly, we all *massively* underestimate just what a huge problem this is – for individuals and for the world we live in. This is a much bigger problem than nearly anyone realizes. In fact, it is arguably the biggest problem of the modern age.

Centuries after we invented the technology of money and financial markets, only a tiny percentage of the population understands them and is using them properly. This is completely crazy. It is a massive tragedy. It is also one of the reasons that life is much harder than it should be for billions of people, and it's a big part of why I wanted to write this book.

Just how stupid this reality is becomes all the more clear when you consider the fact that learning enough about money and finance to make a huge difference to your life and give you a good chance of becoming wealthy is actually no harder than learning how to drive a car.

Lots of people learn how to drive a car. It is a fairly normal thing to do in much of the world. Almost no one learns how to 'drive' their money, however. Imagine if a century after we invented the automobile, only 1–2% of people bothered to learn how to drive one. That would be crazy, right? And a waste of a fantastic technology. Sadly, this is pretty much what we have done with the technology of money and financial markets. Centuries after we invented them, only a tiny percentage of the population has learned about how to use them properly. Funnily enough, these tend to be the people who go on to have more money than the people who don't!

This book will show you how to 'drive' your money. The result is extremely likely to be life-changing.

The final point to stress before we get into the book is that *you* have a truly massive advantage here. As we shall see very soon, when we look at something very important and exciting called 'compounding', *time* is one of the most important factors for your success.

Anyone who learns about money reasonably early in their life has an extremely high chance of becoming a millionaire. I will provide plenty of evidence for this in the pages that follow. The tragedy is that so few people do this.

Far too many people don't even start thinking about or learning about these things until they're in their forties or even later. If you learn about investment – and then start investing yourself – from a young age, you have an incredible advantage. Becoming wealthy will be far easier. This is another 'money secret' that isn't really a secret, just something that too few people know. This stuff is understood by most wealthy people, which is another reason that their children are more likely to be wealthy themselves.

The ultimate point of investing – 'the big picture'

A really important thing to understand before we go on is what the ultimate point of investing is overall. The whole point of investment is:

…getting to a point where you are able to live on your money – or, even better, on the money you make from your money – rather than the money you make from working.

In the language of economists: if you invest, you'll be able to live on your capital, rather than on your labour.

All too often, many people think this concept is incredibly unrealistic, but they really shouldn't. Being able to live on your money, rather than your work, is the reason we invented something called a 'pension'. Hundreds of millions of people, all over the world, have been able to live on their money instead of their work in the century or so since then.

The more you understand about financial markets and investment, the more you will come to realize that this goal is actually entirely attainable.

As long ago as 1996, US investment writers Thomas Stanley and William Danko showed that becoming wealthy is absolutely within reach for most 'normal' people in their bestselling book *The Millionaire Next Door.* They also showed that most millionaires are actually pretty normal people who have made the most of investment throughout their lives.

Another key point to make here is that there are lots of examples of people who have earned a great deal of money in their lives who never learnt about money and finance – and ended up bankrupt as a result.

In the US, this includes some of the most successful celebrities in history, including people like the boxers Mike Tyson and Evander Holyfield; the actors Nicolas Cage, Kim Basinger and Gary Busey; the musicians Toni Braxton, MC Hammer, Willie Nelson and Cyndi Lauper; the tennis star Boris Becker; and even Larry King, one of the most famous American TV hosts of all time.

It has been estimated that a large number of professional footballers in the UK go bankrupt within a few years of the end of their careers. In the US, a large percentage of NFL and NBA players suffer the same fate, even though all of those people were earning six- or even seven-figure salaries a year for many years of their lives.

Amazingly enough, it is also pretty well understood that many lottery winners go bankrupt within a few years of winning the lottery, even though they've often won many millions of dollars or pounds.

So the conclusion here is that being wealthy is far more about knowledge and habit than it is about income. To a great extent, the richest 1% of people in the world are, quite simply, the most financially literate 1% of people in the world. By reading this book, you will significantly increase your chances of being one of them.

Far too many people think that stock market investment and financial markets are 'for rich people' and not for them. This gets things the wrong way round. Investment isn't 'for rich people', it's just that you are far more likely to become a rich person if you learn enough about financial markets and become an investor. There are at least two centuries' worth of evidence that this is the case.

In summary

As we've seen in this introductory chapter, everyone should learn about money. Far from being the 'root of all evil', money is just a technology that has driven human progress for thousands of years. Without it, we would all still be incredibly poor and we wouldn't get to enjoy so many of the wonderful things that make life worth living.

Despite this, very few people have ever learnt about it properly. This has disastrous consequences, and makes people's lives harder than they might otherwise be. By extension, it makes our society worse.

This is particularly tragic given that learning enough about this topic is far easier than most people realize, as we're going to see in this book.

Since time is one of your biggest allies in becoming rich, you have a massive advantage over people who are older than you. Now is the time to learn this stuff!

By understanding money, you will be able to enjoy life far more than if you don't and, arguably even more important, be able to have much more of a positive impact on the world, too.

Happy reading!

PART I

Why you should care (about money and finance)

- What is going on in the world economy today?
- Why do we feel poor when the world is getting richer?
- What are some of the myths about investment, inflation, wealth and the economy?

I

Why you can (and should) learn about saving and investment

'There is an essential life skill that has never been and still isn't taught to the masses: how to manage, control and invest money to protect and provide for your financial future.'

– Mark Shipman, *Big Money, Little Effort* and *EQ v IQ*

Mark Shipman is a British investor and finance author. Mark was able to retire at the age of 35. What I mean by 'retire', is that by the time he turned 35, he was making enough money from his money that he was free to do whatever he wanted to do.

He could spend his time travelling, having fun or playing sports, and be comfortable for the rest of his life. Or he could do something considerably more meaningful like writing or getting involved with charity work.

Either way, the key message here is that it is entirely realistic for you to control your wealth, make a lot of money doing so, and become financially free as a result.

As you read on, we are going to look at how to maximize your chance of becoming wealthy, just like Mark and many others like him, by focusing on what we call our eight fundamental truths of finance.

Our 'owning the world' fundamental truths are:

1 No one is better placed than you to make the most of *your* money.
2 If you learn about money, you have significant advantages over many people who work in finance.
3 Making money from your money (investing) is much easier than many people think. If you can learn how to drive, you can look after your money. It is no harder.
4 You can make far more from your money than you ever thought possible.
5 Eventually, it will be possible for you to make more money from your money than from your job. This is one of the money secrets understood by most rich people.
6 Doing this is possible, no matter how much you earn.
7 The good news: doing this today is easier than ever before. The tools available to you are the most powerful and the cheapest they have ever been.
8 The bad news: it has never been more important to learn about this stuff. It is very unlikely that any government is going to be able to sort this out for you.

Perhaps the best definition of a truly wealthy person is that they are able to live on the money they make from their money, rather than the money they make from working.

Most people aim to get to this point eventually. That's the whole idea of a pension, which is something that we will look at later in the book. It's far less boring than you might think. After all, a pension is just a thing that will (hopefully) ensure you don't have to work for many years of your life!

A big problem today is that far too few people are taking care of this stuff properly. The result of this is that many millions of people are sleepwalking towards being really quite poor later in life. This is something that is relatively easy to avoid, if you learn what you're doing.

Even more exciting, wouldn't it be preferable to get to the point of making a meaningful amount of money from your money years before traditional retirement age?

Life can be far better and much more fun if you're able to create financial freedom many years sooner than your fifties or sixties. The best news is that this is actually possible. You just need to decide right now that you are willing to put a little time in, understand a little bit more than most people do about money and investment, and take the steps required to get yourself sorted.

If you do, you have a far better chance than you ever realized of enjoying genuine financial freedom and doing so in less time than you think.

The fundamental truths given in the list above might seem far-fetched to many people, but I am confident that you will find solid evidence in the pages that follow to back them up.

As you read on, your common sense alone will be enough for you to see the inherent truth in the book's message.

The information that follows will hopefully:

- make you confident in your ability to get your money and finances sorted
- help you learn how to make money from your money, no matter your financial background or what happens in the future
- explain the steps required to make the changes you need to make
- do all of the above in plain English.

Why you must understand what is happening in the world today

We will deal with each of our fundamental truths in turn. In the fine tradition of bad news first, let's get the depressing stuff out of the way as quickly as possible and look at the last one immediately: *it has never been more important for you to learn about this stuff!*

If you don't have a solid understanding of money and finance nowadays, life is likely to get pretty tough. The reason for this is actually quite simple. It has to do with the extent to which governments all over the world are going to struggle to pay people enough to retire on, particularly anyone who is young today.

Although this might seem super-boring and not particularly relevant to anyone under the age of, say, 40, it is actually really important to understand this subject because of the very real effect it is having on all of us and the impact it will have on your life in the years ahead.

Let's explore this in a bit more depth. The US created its 'Social Security' system in 1935. The idea was to provide financial assistance to elderly Americans so that they would be able to survive after they stopped working. The UK had already done something quite similar in 1908, and the same sort of thing happened in many countries all over the world over the course of the 20th century.[1]

Before these various national pension systems were put in place, most people throughout history had to work until they died. This was incredibly tough, as you might imagine. These new systems made life immeasurably better for hundreds of millions of people.

Far from being boring, the creation of these pension systems was one of the most amazing developments for human health and happiness in history. Again, it is important to stress that this would not have been possible without the development of money and financial markets, something which is too little understood and celebrated by people nowadays.

[1] Australia in 1909, Sweden in 1913, France in 1930, Japan in 1942, China in 1951, the Netherlands in 1957, South Korea in 1988 and so on. (Germany was actually first in 1889. Well done, Germany!)

But there is a really key point to understand here. It has to do with the age at which people were able to collect the money as compared to how long people lived.

In the US, for example, the age at which people were entitled to their money from Social Security was set at 65. Crucially, the average life expectancy for a man at the time was around 60 and around 64 for a woman. When the UK system was set up, it was available to the 'elderly poor' over the age of 70. Average life expectancy in the UK at that time, however, was 47 (45 for men and 49 for women), which is amazing if you think about it.

The point here is that the whole system worked because there were lots of workers paying taxes and not that many people who lived long enough to collect an income. You might even accuse these various governments of being a little bit sneaky by deciding to make the retirement age slightly older than the age at which most people died. But there was an important reason that they did this: they wanted to be able to afford to pay the people who did live long enough!

This has completely changed in the time since. Today, many people in the developed world will live into their seventies, eighties or even older. Scientists estimate that this trend is going to continue, with lots of children born nowadays forecast to live to 100 and beyond.

This is a huge problem. In fact, it is arguably the biggest problem of our time, in much of the world at least. It is certainly the biggest problem that hardly anyone talks about. With very few exceptions (Norway, Singapore and Australia, for example), wherever you live in the world today, you absolutely cannot count on being able to live on handouts from your government for the rest of your life after you stop working. It just won't happen, yet most people are relying on exactly those handouts.

That is the bad news, and it really is pretty bad. This is a huge problem facing pretty much every country in the world.

The good news, however, is that you can do something about it. If you understand enough about money and financial markets and take a series of reasonably simple steps, you can realistically expect to become a millionaire – over a long enough period of time at least.

Your minimum goal should be to build a pot of at least one million dollars or pounds by the time you retire. Actually, a far better target would be to achieve this sort of number some years before you reach traditional retirement age, and significantly more by the time you retire, so that you can start enjoying your money much sooner! A million is a pretty random goal, after all. As we go on, you will see that this is entirely possible.

All you have to do for this to happen is read on and…

1 realize that finance is easier to understand than you ever thought. Why do most people never work this out? They never spend any time learning about it! This is one of those strange aspects of human nature. Learning how to run your own financial affairs is a life skill that must rank up there as one of the very best for having a positive impact on all other areas of your life, yet most of us invest our time learning about a vast range of other far less useful life skills and totally neglect finance.
2 learn two amazing facts about finance (Chapter 3)
3 understand two crucial investment themes (Chapter 4)
4 take simple steps to arrange your financial affairs and start making money from your money.

In summary

After you have finished this book, getting your finances in order will very possibly take you less time than you wasted the last time you watched a bad movie. It will certainly take less time than it took you to learn how to drive a car!

As 'repetition is the mother of all learning', let's end this chapter by repeating the quote from Mark Shipman that we started with:

> There is an essential life skill that has never been and still isn't taught to the masses: how to manage, control and invest money to protect and provide for your financial future.

If you learn these skills, not only will you improve your own life, but you'll also put yourself in a position to make a huge difference to the world as well.

Good luck! Reading what follows and acting on it will do nothing less than change your life.

2

Why you can (and should) sort out your own money

'No one cares more about your money than you do. With a basic understanding of the investment process and a bit of discipline, you're perfectly capable of managing your own money… By managing your own money, you'll be able to earn higher returns and save many thousands… in investment costs over your lifetime.'

– Alexander Green, *The Gone Fishin' Portfolio*

Most people do not have confidence in their ability to invest their own money. Be honest – did you spend more time researching the purchase of your last pizza delivery, or pair of trainers or jeans for that matter, than you've ever spent learning the best way to look after your money or reading a solid 'how to invest' book? Do your eyes glaze over when you hear words like 'pensions' or 'shares'?

If you answered 'yes' to both of those questions, don't worry. This is true of lots and lots of people. Crazy as it might sound, this includes many people who work in finance, for reasons we will look at in this chapter.

This is a big shame, because arguably the number one 'secret' of nearly all truly wealthy people is that they *do* understand money and how they can make more money using the money they already have.

Over time, it is actually far easier, quicker and less hassle to have your money (your capital) make money for you than it is to make money from your work (your labour). Whether we like it or not, we live in a capitalist era. One of the fundamental truths of capitalism is that capital tends to make more money than labour. It should be pretty obvious to you that people who *own* businesses tend to make more money than people who work for them. This is truer today than at any other time in history, primarily because capital is more mobile than ever before and can make money all over the world in a huge global market.

Recent research shows that capital's share of the world's overall wealth is the highest relative to labour that it has ever been. This is one of the reasons why the rich people who own businesses are richer than ever relative to people who work for those businesses.

The great news – and this is what far too few people realize – is that the stock market and other forms of investment enable *anyone* to become a business owner. You can own part of some of the best businesses in the world. This is true almost no matter how little money you have to start with. Also, it has never been easier to invest, thanks to inexpensive and powerful online tools that have emerged in the last decade or so.

The fact that making money from money is often easier than making money from work makes sense when you think about the fact that you have a limited number of hours in which to work. Your *money*, on the other hand, 'never sleeps', as the old saying is quite right in telling us.

Money can breed like rabbits if you know what you're doing. Even multimillionaire actors, businesspeople and rock stars have often made a great deal more money from their money than from their performance fees, salaries or record sales.

It is not an exaggeration to say that virtually every very wealthy person in history has made more money from their investments than from being paid for their work. It is also worth noting that they have invariably spent far less time making money from their money than they have from working!

Once your money starts making you money, you will find yourself with the freedom to do anything you want, whether you get paid for your time or not. To become rich, you need to get into this mindset.

The fact that most people do not understand this is a tragedy and one of the reasons so many struggle financially – because they have never properly studied finance, lots of people have really unhelpful beliefs about how money works.

People say things like 'the stock market is a casino'; 'investment is risky'; and 'cash is safe'.

All three of these statements aren't necessarily true in one way or another, a fact that is often well understood by the rich.

The reason many people have come to believe the stock market is a casino is simply because most people know incredibly little about it. Amazingly, this includes many of the people investing in it. Far too many people get involved with investment before they understand almost any of the things that you need to learn before you do.

Investing before you have learnt how to do it properly is a bit like driving a car before you know how to drive: it's dangerous and quite likely to result in you getting hurt! You might be lucky and arrive safely at your destination, but it is more likely that you will have a nasty crash and then tell everyone how dangerous driving is. It is only because so many people involved in financial markets do not know what they are doing that so many lose money and come to believe it is 'risky' or 'a casino'.

Why you can do better than the professionals!

The other big point I want to make in this chapter is that there are a number of reasons why you might be able to do a better job with your own money than many finance professionals do, as mad as that might sound!

When it comes to money and finance, there are a lot of situations in which it makes sense to ask for professional help. This might include arranging a mortgage to buy a home, buying insurance such as health or car cover, help with tax affairs and so on.

In what follows, however, we're going to focus on how useful financial advice is when it concerns *investment* – that is to say, when it comes to *growing your money* as effectively as possible. A key theme in this book is the idea that you are the very best person to take care of this side of things, for a big chunk of your life at least.

Insurance, tax and so on are important, but arguably much less so than getting investment right. It is increasingly easy to take care of lots of financial things ourselves, including insurance and tax, given how many apps and websites there are nowadays. Plenty of online resources, such as financial comparison websites, enable people to do things like buy good-value insurance products and even find the best mortgage rates.

Whether you choose to go down that route or use a financial adviser for these sorts of decisions is obviously entirely up to you. Our key aim here, however, is to make you feel empowered to make your own investment decisions, at the very least.

Ultimately, doing the best job with investment is the most fundamental building block of your personal finances. Saving money is certainly crucial (more on this later), but it is probably worth stressing that most wealthy people focus at least as much, if not more, on investing and growing their money than they do on cutting costs.

Coupon-clipping mums, or the stereotypical dad who turns the heating down in winter, are far less likely to ever become truly wealthy than folk with a more positive and abundant attitude to money. At the simplest level, this is because three hours spent learning about and sorting out your investments will have a much greater impact on your long-term financial situation than three hours spent shaving 20 dollars or pounds off the cost of your car insurance, phone or energy bill. Sadly, too few people think this way. You should become one of them!

So why do I think you could do a better job with investment than lots of financial advisers? There are a number of reasons but arguably the most important among them is the simple fact that financial advisers cost money. Adding another layer of cost onto your investments can make a big difference to how much wealth you build, particularly over many years.

We will see in a bit more detail why this is when we look at something called 'compound interest' in the next chapter, but the basic point is that the long-run impact of reducing your investment returns can be pretty large.

To give a simple example, imagine a 25-year-old who is lucky enough to have $10,000 to invest. Imagine they keep that money invested until they turn 65. To keep the maths easy, if they were to make 10% a year, they would have just under $452,593 by the time they turned 65!

If they paid a financial adviser 1% a year along the way, however, their real return after that cost would be 9% annually. Amazingly enough, this would reduce what they have when they turn 65 to just over $314,000! A cost of 'only' 1% (which is what good financial advice will cost you in many parts of the world), will have reduced the amount of money they've been able to build by more than $138,000 over a lifetime of investment!

This example only assumes a single one-time investment of $10,000. Of course, in the real world, you will be investing money every month for decades, which means the difference can end up being very big indeed – possibly even seven figures for a high earner.

That having been said, it is important to stress that you will only get this benefit if you learn enough about finance to do a good job with your own finances. There is actually a good deal of evidence that the average person who has used a financial adviser ends up with more money than the average person who doesn't or retires earlier. It is important to understand, however, that people who use financial advisers tend to be those with higher incomes who are more focused on saving and investment.

What this means, in summary, is that the best thing to be is a well-informed amateur or 'DIY' investor. If you know enough to do a good job so that you don't have to pay a financial adviser, you will be in a real investing 'sweet spot'.

Hopefully you find this exciting. What is even more exciting is that learning how to get into that sweet spot is not as hard as you think. Reading this book should get you most of the way there.

One final point to make here is that you might consider using a financial adviser as you get older. This is because most people's finances get more complicated as they get older. Plus, you should have quite a lot more money by then, so the downside of getting things wrong could be more extreme (a topic to which we will return to later in the book).

The 'set and forget' approach to building wealth we cover in this book is intended to be as simple to follow as possible and very much aimed at growing your money. If you really get to grips with it, you should be able to do a pretty good job with your money for many years, and certainly in your twenties and thirties. If you decide to get a financial adviser after that, you'll have saved yourself many years of fees. Whatever you decide in the years ahead, you will be in a much stronger position and also be far better placed to know how to choose a good financial adviser when the time comes.

In the rest of this section of the book we'll begin to look at more of the key things you will want to understand to ensure that you're able to do a great job with your money for many years.

3
Two amazing facts about finance

'Those who understand compound interest are destined to collect it. Those who don't are doomed to pay it.'

– Tom and David Gardner, founders of The Motley Fool (www.fool.co.uk)

In this chapter we look at 'two amazing facts about finance'. Both of them will give you an idea of how exciting sorting your money out can be. These two things are:

1 Something called 'compound interest' or 'compounding'.
2 The fact that financial products and services today are the best they've ever been.

Let's look at each of these in turn.

Amazing fact 1: Compound interest – 'the eighth wonder of the world'

If you take nothing more away from this book than an understanding of the incredible power of compound interest, or compounding, then you will have joined a lucky (and generally wealthy) few.

Compounding is arguably the single most important thing you will ever learn about money and finance. In fact, you might argue that the whole idea is one of the most important things to learn in *life* more generally – something we will look at a bit later in the chapter.

Compounding is the reason investment can be so powerful. As we will see, it can turn a few hundred dollars or pounds invested regularly over your adult life into more than a million.

For what it is worth, you can find a fair bit online suggesting that no less a figure than Albert Einstein was pretty keen on the idea of compounding. Things he is rumoured to have said about it include:

> Compound interest is the most powerful force in the universe

… and…

> Compound interest is the Eighth Wonder of the World.

When he was asked to name the greatest invention in human history, his answer was: 'Compound interest'.

If you spend a bit of time googling this stuff, you'll see various fact-checking websites that call into question whether he ever said any of this. Nevertheless, as another top investor has put it:

'Whether or not he really said it – I strongly suggest you adopt the idea…'

I would certainly agree with this position, given how life-changing compound interest can be. So let's look at it in more detail.

In some ways, you might think of compounding as a form of *free money*… and it is money that grows like a weed over time. But how can this be?

Well, imagine that you invested £1,000 today. Imagine, too, that whatever you invested it in went up by 10% this year. (By the way, if you think this sort of return is unrealistic, it is worth noting that American shares have averaged more than 10% a year in the *century* from 1923 to the time of writing.)

In this scenario, if you've made 10% you would then have £1,100 one year after your initial investment – your original sum, plus £100 of investment return.[1] Simple so far. Now comes the free money part. Assume you invested that £1,100 for another year and achieved 10% again. The following year you would have £1,210. This time you've made £110 of return (£1,100 × 1.1 = £1,210). Crucially, £10 of that return is essentially *free money*. It is the *return on your return*.

At first glance this may not seem particularly exciting, but over time the effect is incredibly powerful. Let's look more closely at some examples.

If one dollar invested today achieves long-run stock market returns of around 7.5% (after inflation), after 20 years, that dollar would have become nearly $4.25; after 30 years, nearly $8.75; and after 40 years just over $18!

The US stock market actually returned an average of 10.46% in the century from January 1923 to December 2023. One dollar invested at that rate of return would be $7.31 after 20 years, nearly $20 after 30 years, and more than $53 after 40 years.

Put another way – the £1,000 television that a 25-year-old might buy could rob their 65-year-old self of somewhere between £18,000 and £53,000. Or, perhaps illustrated even more powerfully, that sort

[1] £1,000 × 1.1 = £1,100.

of investment return could turn £10,000 into somewhere between £180,000 and £530,000 over a lifetime of investing from your twenties to your sixties.

Time is key: $5,000 becomes nearly $1 million

Here's another example of how powerful this can be. Imagine a grandparent or wealthy relative was able to invest $5,000 the day a child is born. Now imagine that investment achieves 10% a year until that child retires.

With no further investment at all, that initial sum would have grown to around $1 million by the time the child turned 55 and nearly $2.5 million by the time they turn 65.

It is worth really dwelling on these numbers for a moment. This is how powerful an effect compounding can have over many years. It shows just how important it is to understand it properly.

A key point to make here is just how few people do understand this stuff. Surveys in both the US[2] and the UK[3] have shown that more than 60% of the adult population doesn't understand compounding (the way that you do now!).

This is a huge tragedy. It is arguably one of the main reasons that most people do not make the most of their money. Because so many people don't understand the concept, they don't believe in the amazing power of compounding to have a truly life-changing effect on their wealth and their life.

It probably goes without saying that people who believe they have half a chance of turning hundreds of pounds or dollars into millions of pounds or dollars over time are far more likely to invest. People who don't understand compounding and who don't, therefore, believe in this potential are far more likely to do nothing.

This is one of the key reasons why so few people are investing. I would argue that this is one of the biggest tragedies of our time.

---

[2] https://www.cnbc.com/2019/02/11/how-compound-interest-works-and-how-it-can-help-you-save-money.html

[3] https://www.aviva.com/newsroom/news-releases/2023/04/effect-of-inflation-on-savings-not-understood-by-majority-of-brits/

It is absolutely crucial to understand and believe in the power of compounding if you want to become wealthy.

Try not to borrow money!

Another really important point to make here is that compounding works both ways. What I mean by this is that if you *borrow* money, the amount of money you owe (your debt) will almost certainly grow a great deal faster than if you save and invest money. This is another thing that far too few people understand, often with really painful and tragic results.

When you borrow money, the interest rate you are charged on that money will almost always be higher than the interest rate you will be paid if you save or invest your money. More often than not it will be a lot higher!

At the time of writing, if you save money in a decent savings account of some kind, you will be lucky to earn around 4–5% on your money. If you invest your money in the stock market, over long periods of time you might make somewhere between 7% and 10%. If you borrow money on a credit card, however, you're likely to have to *pay* 20% or even 25% in interest on that money.

To give an example of how extreme the difference between saving and investing, on the one hand, and borrowing, on the other, can be, let's compare saving and investing £5,000 for five years at roughly stock market rates of return to borrowing £5,000 and paying around the current average APR (Annual Percentage Rate) on a credit card of around 23%.

If you save and invest £5,000 for five years and make a 5% return you would have nearly £6,400. If you were able to make 10% by investing that money, you would have more than £8,000. If you had borrowed that same £5,000 on a credit card at an APR of 23%, however, you would now have more than £14,000 of debt. We've shown the difference between making 10% and borrowing at 23% in the graph below. After only five years you could be more than £20,000 poorer if you borrow versus save and invest.

As you can see, this is quite a big difference. Debt almost always compounds *against* you far more powerfully than saving or investing

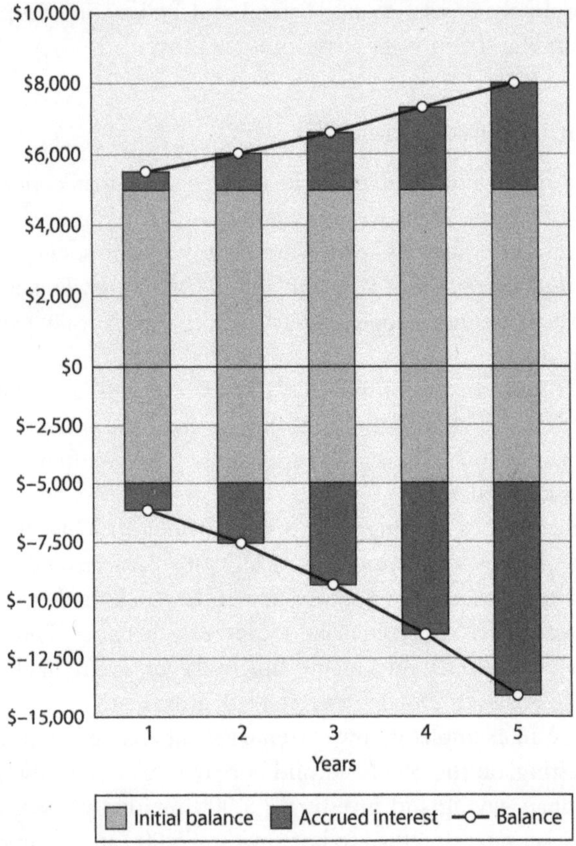

FIGURE 1 The difference between investing and borrowing

compounds *for* you, particularly when it comes to credit card debt or things like store loans, which usually charge high interest rates. You can see what a big difference it makes after only five years. Make no bones about it: over a lifetime, compounding one way or the other will make the difference between struggling financially and having the potential to become reasonably wealthy.

The fact that more than 60% of people don't understand this stuff is a big part of why so many people have such a hard time financially.

As you go through life it is a really good idea to be very careful about using debt. If you play your cards right, you might even be able to avoid using it altogether, although this could be difficult, particularly when you're young.

The key point, however, is to make sure you don't lose control and get yourself into trouble with debt. If you do that, it can take years to pay back, which can be extremely unpleasant and stressful, and you are far less likely to be become wealthy as a result.

Compounding and inequality

It is worth spending a moment to explain another aspect of compounding that is very poorly understood. This is the fact that compounding is also a big part of why there is inequality in the world.

To explain why this is, let's conduct a simple thought experiment. Imagine two friends who start with the same amount of money in their early twenties. Imagine they also have roughly the same education, skills, work ethic, health and fitness, and so on.

Now imagine that one of them gets roughly 1% 'better' in their life each and every month and *only* 1% better. They read an extra book, work a bit harder in their day job, spend a little bit more time in the gym, eat slightly better food, and learn a bit about financial markets.

Now imagine that this translates over time into them being able to earn a little more. Imagine that they are able to grow their wealth by about 1% a month too throughout their life as a result.

Each of them has $1,000 at the age of 25. The friend who makes no progress at all spends all of his or her money each year and still has $1,000 the following year. Now consider what happens to these two friends over 40 years; from the age of 25 to 65.

Crucially, mathematically, the one who gets *only* 1% better each month will have turned that $1,000 into $118,648, as compared to the other friend who still only has $1,000.

The key point to make here is that the difference over 40 years isn't that one of the friends is a *little bit* wealthier because they did 1% better each month. They are nearly *119 times* wealthier! This isn't some kind of nasty conspiracy theory. This is just how the mathematics of compounding works. It's so important to understand this.

You might argue that this is a silly economists' thought experiment that's not very realistic. In reality, the differences will likely be far larger. In real life the difference between our two friends could be far more than in the example given above. This is because the sums involved will likely be far more than just $1,000. Plus, the sort of person who pushes themselves onto the trajectory of getting only a little bit better and wealthier every month will very likely continue to improve over time, and the gap will widen still further.

If you change the assumption to 2% better each month, they would be 13,400 times wealthier. If you made it 3%, they would be nearly 1.5 *million* times wealthier.[4]

You might also add a third friend to the thought experiment. The third friend is someone who never reads a book, takes no exercise, eats really badly, never learns anything about finance, and gets themselves into a lot of debt at a young age. Over several decades, this person is going to end up being massively worse off than their friend who gets only 1% better each month.

One of the most important things to understand here is that you won't see much of a difference between these three friends at the age of, say, 30. One of them might have a slightly better job and be in slightly better shape and so on. By the age of 50 and beyond, however, their respective life outcomes will be enormously different. This is just how the mathematics of compounding works.

It is for this reason that I would argue that the whole idea of compounding could actually be one of the single most important things anyone will ever learn. People who work in finance tend to be in the minority of the population who understand such things, because it is a core requirement of their job. The bigger point, however, is the impact compounding has on your *life*, not just on your money.[5]

Now that you understand more about compounding than most people, you're in a much better place to make sure you can benefit

---

[4] If you want to check the calculations here, please use this excellent website: https://www.thecalculatorsite.com/finance/calculators/compound-interestcalculator.php

[5] A great book on this subject is *The Slight Edge* by Jeff Olson.

from it as 'the most powerful force in the universe', at least so far as wealth, success and happiness are concerned.

Slow and steady wins the race...

As you should be able to see from the examples we've just gone through, time is your biggest ally when it comes to building wealth. Small amounts of money can turn into very large amounts of money over a long enough period of time. This is one of the most important things anyone will ever learn about becoming wealthy.

One of the main objections I hear when sharing my excitement about the wonderful world of investing is: 'But that won't work for me, I don't have enough money to invest.' This is almost always not true. You can start with very little. Even tiny amounts can make a huge difference, particularly if you start as early in life as possible – as you can!

Too many people believe that they need a big lump sum or the ability to save a large amount of money every month to make investment worthwhile.

Too many also believe that investment is 'for the rich' and not for them. The reality is the other way around. Investing isn't 'for the rich'. It's just that if you learn about money and investment, you're far more likely to be rich!

With money, as with so many things in life, knowledge is power. It is also the tortoise who generally wins the race, not the hare. You are much more likely to save a small amount of money right now than you are to save a large amount of money at some time in the future. I'm sure you are familiar with this psychology. It is also true of going to the gym, revising for exams, doing housework and so on. The longer you leave your dishes in the sink, the bigger a job tidying the kitchen becomes. The longer you go without exercising, the harder exercising becomes. The longer you put off investing, the harder it will be to become wealthy.

Since time is one of the most important factors in whether you can become wealthy or not, you must take action now – or as soon as possible. Start small but start now. If you do start small, no matter how small, you will enable yourself to benefit from the magic of compounding, and this can and will make a huge difference to your fortunes in the years ahead.

In investment, slow, steady and consistent wins the race and small numbers add up to very big numbers over time. So try and get at least *some* money to work as soon as you can!

This brings us to our next big idea – the fact that it has never been easier to do this.

Amazing fact 2: Financial products and services are the best they've ever been

As we've already seen, far too few people get a proper education about money. As a result, far too few people save and invest. All over the developed world, surveys tell us that most people have very little money saved and more than half of the adult population isn't investing. This is a huge shame when you consider the fact that it has never been easier or cheaper to become an investor.

In recent decades there have been lots of very interesting developments in the finance industry. Today's financial world offers you more tools than ever before. Thanks to advances in technology, there are now tonnes of financial products and services available to you that are designed to make understanding, managing and growing your money easier, faster and cheaper than ever before.

Budgeting and saving apps can help you see exactly where your money goes each month, help you set savings goals, and automate saving and investment. Not that long ago, all of this required far more work when compared to everything you can do with a few taps on your phone nowadays.

It has also never been easier to invest. One of the biggest advantages of all this progress is that you can start investing and growing your wealth with very small amounts of money. Gone are the days when investing was only for people with lots of money. Advanced investment apps enable you to invest automatically every month, and buy fractions of shares and other assets, meaning you can build wealth with as little as a few dollars, pounds or euros each month.

Plus, because information about investing is more accessible than ever, it is easier than ever before to learn the basics, either from your app provider, YouTube, social media, financial blogs – or books like this one of course! You don't have to be an expert or have a lot of money to start investing, and over time, small amounts can turn into much bigger ones thanks to compounding, as we have just seen.

Today's financial products are also often built with younger users in mind. Many of them focus on financial education and making smart choices, over and above providing you with the tools you need to get your money working for you.

Whether it's learning about budgeting, managing debt or investing, there's a good chance you'll find apps and services that break down these concepts in simple, engaging ways. Not only do these tools make managing money easier, but they also help build the knowledge and habits that will benefit you throughout your whole life. With a bit of curiosity and the right tools, you can set yourself up for a strong financial future, even if you're just getting started.

This used to be much harder. If you wanted to build wealth, you needed quite a lot of money to begin with; there was a great deal of admin to do; and the costs were a great deal higher than they are today. In the last few years, thanks to the internet and intense innovation from financial services companies around the world, these hurdles have pretty much disappeared. As a result, investing is far simpler for us than it was for our parents or grandparents. This is pretty exciting when you think about it.

Moving swiftly on...

So now you are up to speed on the power of compound interest and the fact that it is easier than ever before to save and invest. Knowing these two facts alone gives you a huge advantage over most people.

Now we shall turn our attention to two incredibly important, big-picture investment themes which can really help you get your money working for you.

4
Two crucial investment themes

'Barring the cataclysmic unforeseen, the outlook for business is good and will become even better as time goes on.'

– John Paul Getty, *How to be Rich*

This quote comes from the late John Paul Getty, who was once the richest living American – and, in the mid-1960s became the richest person in the entire world. He made this comment during the Great Depression (c.1929–39), when many people felt as pessimistic about the state of the world and their own financial situation as they do today.

His quote probably seemed crazy to most people at the time, but by now he has been right for nearly a century.

What you need to know about economic growth and inflation

This chapter is where things get quite exciting. If you got your head around the two amazing facts in the previous chapter, and can get to grips with the two key themes discussed in this one, then your knowledge of finance will quite literally be in the top tiny percentage of people in the world and you will be very well placed to become wealthy as a result!

Our two crucial themes are:

1 The world keeps on growing: when you think about becoming wealthy, it's best to ignore any thoughts of financial crises or recessions. The fact is that, throughout your life, it is very likely that the world as a whole will continue to grow and develop. If you are invested in this idea, you will benefit in a big way.

   As Warren Buffett, arguably the world's most famous living investor, has put it: 'There is always a bull market somewhere'. Or, as I like to say: 'Human progress is the most important investment theme in history.'

2 There is significant inflation in the world: at the same time that the world is growing, and partly related to that fact, there is quite a lot of a nasty thing called 'inflation' going on in most parts of the world. It is really important to understand this reality if you want to become wealthy.

Let's look at each of these crucial investment themes in turn:

Theme 1: The world economy keeps on growing

The world is much richer today than it was ten years ago, and certainly much richer than it was 20, 50 or 100 years ago. In fact, even just the last decade or so has seen human beings produce something like 25% of all the wealth ever created in the whole of human history!

To illustrate how powerful this is: as near as we can calculate it, the world economy as a whole was worth about $12.5 trillion in 1985. By the end of 2021, this number had grown to $96.3 trillion. That is to say that the global economy as a whole had grown by around 670%! It is forecast to continue to grow to nearly $135 trillion by the end of 2028.

This has happened at the same time that we've had big stock market crashes such as the 'dot-com crash' in the late 1990s, and the 'global financial crisis' of 2007–9. We've also had COVID-19 to deal with and countless other pretty awful things going on such as the wars in Ukraine and the Middle East.

Despite all of these worrying developments, the world has continued to grow and grow. This is because of the power of human progress overall. This is one of the most important things to understand about money, finance and investment. It's helpful to remind yourself of this as you get your money to work.

Nearly all of us carry a device around with us every day which is far more powerful than the computer that put a man on the moon just over half a century ago. That device (your smartphone) can give you access to almost any information you can think of in less than a minute. You can listen to pretty much any song or read pretty much any book on demand. You can make audio or video calls to people on the other side of the world for free. It's a diary, camera, fitness instructor, dietician, radio, torch, map, tour guide, watch, magazine and newspaper and a whole constellation of other things. Plenty of people even run multi-million-dollar businesses from a smart phone.

If you are a fan of science fiction, you might have heard of the famous novel and film *2001: A Space Odyssey*. Sir Arthur C. Clarke, the British author who wrote that book, famously said:

> Any sufficiently advanced technology is indistinguishable from magic.

If you showed an iPhone or Samsung Galaxy to someone from the late 1990s (let alone the 1940s or 1880s), it would look like something incredibly magical to them – like something out of *Star Trek*. Yet, today it is something that billions of us take entirely for granted. It seems pretty ordinary.

The same can be said of lots of other things. Cars are better. Planes are better. Global travel has massively increased. Comfortably more than a billion people have been lifted out of poverty in the last few decades, and the world is actually, factually the most peaceful and abundant it has ever been in history *by far*.

Very importantly, anyone who has been *invested* in these developments will have had a pretty good chance of becoming wealthy. The 'magic' of a smartphone, which would be so mind-blowing to that person from the 1990s, has created several trillion dollars of real wealth in the last quarter century. This kind of thing is more than likely to continue in future if the last two centuries of history is anything to go by. Overall, human beings are the richest they have ever been, and the world will very likely continue to get even richer, because of population growth and economic and technological development.

This is one of the most important things to understand and believe in if you want to become wealthy.

What about the environment, though?!

Of course, if you care about the environment, you might find all this growth quite worrying. After all, the more the world's population and economy grows, the more energy and raw materials we use, and the more pollution and waste we create.

But a key point to make here is that it *is* actually entirely possible for us to have economic growth and improve our environment. There are actually lots of examples of this going on in the world already, much of which is poorly understood, and almost none of which gets enough press, for reasons we will get to in a moment.

Take cars for example: the fuel efficiency of cars and trucks has improved enormously in the last few decades. The average car or truck today covers nearly twice as many 'miles per gallon' (MPG) as they did a generation ago. Then there are electric vehicles, of course, or EVs for short. The share of electric cars has increased from only 4% of the global car market as recently as 2020 to more than 18% in 2023.[1]

Arguably just as exciting, are car-sharing companies like Zipcar, Getaround and Turo, which you may have heard of. These are companies that use clever apps so that you can pick up a car, use it for a few hours, and only pay for the time you use, meaning that you may not need to own your own car.

This is particularly good news when you consider that the average car sits outside, unused for about 22 hours a day, and that when most cars are actually being driven, there tend to be at least three empty seats – which is all very inefficient and bad for the environment.

It has been estimated that there could be as many as one million 'shared' cars on the road by 2027 and that each of them can replace 4–8 personally owned cars; some estimates put the number much higher than this.[2] Given the rate at which these sorts of companies are growing, it won't be that long before we need tens of millions fewer cars in the world, and eventually even hundreds of millions fewer.

Then there are companies like Uber and Lyft. Uber is now the biggest taxi company in the world, operating in more than 10,000 cities in nearly 100 countries. Because of the way that drivers and passengers can use the app to match demand and supply, Uber, and lots of other companies like it, use cars more efficiently than the taxi companies of the past.

Similarly, Airbnb is the biggest accommodation company in the world today, much larger than even the very biggest hotel chains. You might argue that the fact that Airbnb makes use of existing buildings makes it more efficient and better for the environment than building great big new hotels all over the place. It didn't even exist as recently as 20 years ago.

Uber and Airbnb are both very big companies, meaning that they have created a great deal of economic growth along the way. These sorts of businesses allow us to do something called 'collaborative

[1] https://www.iea.org/energy-system/transport/electric-vehicles

[2] https://www.globalfleet.com/en/tags/car-sharing

consumption'. This means that we are increasingly able to rent and share things using clever apps, instead of having to buy them. We can also make far more use of things (like cars or buildings) that exist already, rather than having to make so many new ones.

Nowadays, there are businesses that enable you to rent all sorts of things, including expensive clothes or jewellery for a special occasion, or products like garden tools. This is great news when you consider the environmental impact of 'fast fashion', and also the fact that the average lawn mower is only used for about four hours a year, and the average power drill for 22 minutes in its entire lifespan! Advances in our IT systems and apps will hopefully mean that there is a great deal more of this collaborative consumption in the years ahead across a wide range of the things we do.

There are also charities and apps that help us to recycle food so it doesn't go to waste, and the second-hand market for everything is many times bigger today than it was in the past thanks to companies like eBay, Amazon and Facebook Marketplace. In fact, the second-hand market is currently worth several hundred billion dollars and is growing at around 13% a year. This is likely to be very good news for the environment and for the future, not least given how many of these developments are actually still in the relatively early stages of their development.

Urbanization and efficiency

One of the biggest themes of the last century is something called 'urbanization'. This just means that more and more of us all over the world are living in cities. In 1900, only about 15% of human beings lived in cities. Today, more than half of us do, and it is estimated that this trend will continue and this number will continue to grow.

Urbanization is really helpful for growth in all of these collaborative consumption and sharing trends. When people live more closely together, it is a great deal easier to share things and buy and sell things in a second-hand market. Owning property and cars also tends to be much more expensive in cities, which makes people more likely to think about renting. There is also a good deal of evidence that people who live in cities tend to think more about waste and pollution, given how much more visible such problems are in a city as compared to in the countryside.

Happily, we are getting steadily more efficient in how we use resources even when it comes to building and making *new* things as well. We've already shown how cars and trucks get far better mileage for every gallon of fuel. The same sort of thing has been true across all sorts of industrial processes.

The aluminium cans we get our favourite drinks in are a good example of this. Thanks to advances in materials science, since the 1970s the amount of metal we use in each can has fallen by around 40% and, today, more than 70% of the metal we do use is recycled.

Dematerialization

Another encouraging thing to highlight is something called 'dematerialization'. This is all about shifting away from physical formats to digital formats. To give a good example of this: not that long ago, if you wanted to listen to music or watch a movie, you needed a CD or DVD. A few years before that, you would have had to have a cassette, VHS video tape or vinyl record.

Today, almost all of this resource-hungry activity has been replaced by virtual, on-line, on-demand streaming services, played using our smart phones or computers, or on televisions that are infinitely thinner and lighter than the monster TVs that our parents had! Digital streaming services eliminate the need for the physical production and transportation of media, which has hugely reduced the environmental impact of the entertainment industry. This has all happened very quickly. Of course, these new technologies *do* use lots of electricity, but the industry has become steadily more efficient over the years as well, with many data centres now running on renewable energy. There are reasons to believe that this will get even better in the future, as we shall see in the next few pages.

Our Future is Biotech

If you're reading this book, you may know that my last book was called *Our Future is Biotech*. It's all about the biotechnology sector.

In researching that book I came across all sorts of really exciting technologies that could have a role to play in helping us achieve economic growth without wrecking the planet!

For example, we are probably not that many years away from being able to replace all our nasty, polluting plastics with alternative materials that come from natural, renewable resources. Biotech companies are researching and developing biodegradable materials that come from things like plant starches, cellulose and algae.

Products made from these materials will very likely provide us with the same functionality as the plastic things they'll replace. Unlike plastics, though, after they're used, they'll break down into harmless natural components that don't cause pollution. We may even be able to effectively 'grow' such things in the fullness of time. This will reduce our consumption of oil and gas, which are the main raw materials required to make plastics.

Similarly exciting, there are lots of these sorts of technologies which are going to be able to repair much of the damage we have done to the planet in the last couple of centuries since the Industrial Revolution. 'Bioremediation' is a word that describes how we can use certain living organisms, such as bacteria, plants and fungi to detoxify and remove contaminants from our environment.

These technologies can break down a wide range of harmful pollutants, such as heavy metals in our soils and plastics in our oceans, seas, lakes and rivers, often into completely non-toxic end products. As this sort of science develops, these approaches will become far less expensive and more environmentally sustainable than anything we had at our disposal in the past. They may even one day enable us to completely repair parts of the world which were previously very polluted.

Another example of an exciting technology that could be really helpful to the environment within our lifetimes is 'DNA storage'. You probably know that DNA[3] is found in nearly all living things and is sometimes called the 'life molecule'. Without wanting to get too technical, DNA is able to store the code of life. Your DNA stores all of the instructions for things like your hair, eye and skin colour – and a huge amount else besides.

[3] DNA stands for 'deoxyribonucleic acid'.

The main point here is that a single cell's worth of DNA stores an incredible amount of information. Scientists have realized that we could potentially take advantage of this fact to develop DNA as a storage technology to replace things like hard drives, magnetic tapes and servers. A single gram of DNA could store as much as 215 million gigabytes of data. All the data we have ever created as a species so far in history could fit in something the size of a small truck![4]

Perhaps even more exciting, this technology may not need any power! Once the DNA is 'coded' with the information, it could be stored on a shelf at room temperature, just like a book, as compared to a hard drive or server, which needs lots of power. DNA is also incredibly durable and can last for hundreds, thousands, or quite possibly even millions of years, when you consider that we have been able to analyse DNA that came from a mammoth that was over one million years old.

Can you imagine just how much electricity we will be able to save across the world if all our storage technologies can be grown in a lab, don't need any power, and can last for thousands of years?

There are lots of exciting developments just around the corner that will mean that the economy can grow *and* we can do a much better job with respect to our environment at the same time. This is because lots of the economic growth in humanity's future will come from companies working on all of the technologies we've just looked at, and lots of others too. If you start to look into such things, you will get a powerful sense of the incredible progress we are already making.

Fewer human beings?

Another factor here is that, contrary to what all too many people believe, the global population is very likely to stop rising and actually start *falling* in the years ahead, for the first time since the Industrial Revolution. Many years' worth of evidence shows that the richer and more developed a country becomes, the fewer children people choose to have. This decline in birth rates is due to all sorts of things, many of which have to do with capital markets, as we shall see.

[4] https://www.micron.com/about/blog/applications/data-center/dnas-awesome-potential-to-store-the-worlds-data

If you take out the impact of immigration, the population of many of the most developed countries has been shrinking for years. Between 2000 and 2020, Germany's population would have shrunk by more than 5 million people, had they not had several million immigrants enter the country from places like Turkey and Africa. Italy would have lost more than 1.5 million. The same has been true in Switzerland, Scandinavia and lots of other European countries.

Even with more than a million immigrants in that same time frame, Japan's population overall has still shrunk by more than a million, and Romania has lost nearly 2.5 million people![5] The population of South Korea today is just over 50 million, but is forecast to fall to below 40 million in the next 30 years or so as fewer Koreans are deciding to get married and have children.

Many smart writers and thinkers now believe that the world's population could peak as soon as the middle of this century and then start going into reverse. The change could actually happen quite quickly as birth rates fall. Some people worry that this could be very challenging for our economic model, which has been based on population growth for the last couple of centuries. Plenty of others, however, believe that we may be able to look forward to a fairly bright future with fewer, richer people, doing far less damage to the planet.

There is a good chance that technological innovation, such as advances in robotics for example, over and above the developments we've already looked at, and so many others, will mean that there can be fewer workers and much higher wages. This should be very good for our environment, for the planet, and for our species overall, as we can all live wealthier, happier, healthier and longer lives.

What did financial markets ever do for us?

A key point to make here is that we have financial markets to thank for most of the progress we have made so far in history. Crucially,

[5] https://www.pewresearch.org/short-reads/2024/07/08/in-some-countries-immigration-accounted-for-all-population-growth-between-2000-and-2020/

financial markets are also one of the most important things which will help us deliver all of the exciting stuff we've just looked at in this chapter, which can and will significantly improve our world.

Sadly, this is a point that is all too poorly understood by 'anti-capitalists'. It is very likely that capitalistic companies and financial markets will be best placed to deliver the result we all want and need here. There are already thousands of companies all over the world working on the technologies we need to solve most of our problems. Many critics don't seem to be aware of the incredible progress being made by such companies, or even that they exist.

To move as quickly as possible into a brighter future in which we can all live wealthier lives, and repair our planet at the same time, we need to make sure there is the money (capital) available for these companies to do the best job they can. Tearing down the system with no good idea about how to replace it is almost certainly going to slow down the progress we need to make – or, more likely, stop it altogether. It's so important that more people understand such things, and part of the reason I wanted to write this book!

The other thing worth mentioning in passing here is that we also have capital markets to thank for that declining population trend. Traditionally, the reason that people in developing countries tended to have lots of children is because families relied on their children and grandchildren to support them and look after them in old age. In countries with no pension system or any other similar safety nets, such as employment benefits or social security, the only people who are going to look after you when you get old are your family. Sadly, even today, a fair number of children in such countries also die when they are young because of disease, starvation or war. This means people tend to want to have even more children, given the risk that not all of them will survive.

This is why birth rates in the poorest countries in the world are still so high. In many sub-Saharan African countries,[6] the 'fertility rate' (the average number of children per woman) is still more than five or even six. This is a big reason why these countries have such a low

[6] Niger, Angola, Congo, Mali, Chad, Uganda and Somalia, for example.

average income and so many people are extremely poor. These are very small, unproductive economies, with large and growing populations. If your economy doesn't grow, but you have millions more mouths to feed every few years, everyone becomes steadily poorer over time.

As countries develop economically and introduce widespread safety nets, particularly pension systems so that elderly folks can still have an income when they stop working, people no longer need to have lots of children.

This is what has happened in western Europe, the US and much of Asia in the last few decades. With fewer children and growing economies, people can get richer; much richer, in fact. The best examples of this are in Asian countries like Taiwan, South Korea and Singapore, where advanced pension systems were developed in the last century, birth rates fell a long way, and average incomes have risen fantastically.

At the end of the Second World War, Taiwan and South Korea were two of the poorest countries in the world, poorer even than many sub-Saharan African countries. Today, they are two of the richest countries in the world in terms of the average income and wealth of their citizens. This has a great deal to do with how their pension systems and capital markets developed and has happened pretty quickly when you think about it.

Given the very positive trajectory of these countries, it is exciting to note that the birth rate in India has fallen from more than six children per woman in the 1950s to around two today. This bodes well for average incomes in India (as well as for resource and energy consumption, and pollution and waste too of course). This is a big part of why India is so often described as enjoying a kind of economic miracle. Similarly, Iranian women are having about two children each on average today versus more than six as recently as the 1980s. This could be very positive for Iran's development and income levels in the years ahead.

All the things we've covered over these last few pages could have a tremendous impact on our future. Human ingenuity and scientific progress, funded by capital markets, have a decent shot at enabling the whole world to grow economically without destroying our planet.

Q: Why don't we ever hear about this stuff?
A: Negative press bias!

Before we move on to the next section of the book, it's worth thinking about why so few people know about the things we've just covered. The main reason is actually quite simple. It is because of something called 'negative press bias'.

It's a well-established fact that wherever you live in the world, the vast majority of 'the news' that you are presented with every day on TV, on the radio, in the newspapers and from mainstream online sources has a very significant *negative bias*. This is to say that it is very strongly focused on bad news, and good news hardly gets a look in. The same is generally true of social media, as you will no doubt be painfully aware. If you are lucky, there might be a light-hearted story about a water-skiing squirrel right at the end of your nightly television news bulletin, but that's the exception that proves the rule.

The next time you watch the news, please do take a moment to really focus on the percentage of stories that concern something exceptionally awful, as opposed to the percentage focused on anything even vaguely positive. Every day you are bombarded with stories about war, famine, murder, disease, political corruption and so much else besides. Very rarely will you see an uplifting, positive piece about transformational new technologies, or any of the wonderful progress we are actually making.

You might argue that this is all pretty strange and more than a little silly. A large percentage of the population all over the world will come home in the evening, slump in front of the television and choose to watch someone in a dark suit spend half an hour telling them about all of the really terrible things that happened in the world today, and pretty much *only* those terrible things. Most of those things will also have taken place thousands of miles away from where that person lives, and will more than likely have little or no real impact on their day-to-day lives.

Many people spend significant chunks of their time doing much the same thing on their smartphones as they go about their day. This is seen as entirely normal. People think they are 'informed' as a result of this behaviour. In fact, they have an extremely distorted idea of the true state of the world.

The reason that our news is the way it is has to do with how our psychology functions at a fundamental level, how this impacts all of us as the audience for news, and how journalists, editors and media companies behave as a result.

The problem is that we human beings have some extraordinarily problematic 'software' in our brains. We are hard-wired psychologically to focus on the extraordinary (and negative), and not on the unremarkable (and positive).

To be fair to all of us, there is a reason our brains work this way. For most of human history, people were very poor and resources were scarce. The world was also much more dangerous than it is today. Our ancestors had to be far more careful about wild animals and other human beings than we need to be today, and so it benefitted them to expect the worst. Catastrophic thinking was a key survival mechanism, and so our brains developed to be far more focused on negative, dangerous things over many thousands of years.

Sadly, even though the world today is far more peaceful, safe and abundant, our brains are still built for the much more dangerous reality that most human beings had to deal with in the past.

Journalists and news editors know this, which is why they lean in to doom and gloom. This is what sells copy and drives clicks – because we are all hard-wired to pay attention to exactly that kind of content.

'If it bleeds, it leads' has been a famous saying in newsrooms all over the world for many decades. Sadly, really awful things like war, murder, school shootings and so on sell far more newspapers and drive more clicks – and bring business to media companies – than positive news about the great progress we are making scientifically, for example.

Perhaps of most relevance to this book, this reality is also one of the reasons that so many people fail to learn about money and financial markets and become wealthy. This is because this strong inherent negative bias extends to the coverage of financial markets, too.

A financial market crash of any kind will be all over our newspapers and will headline TV news bulletins. The slow and steady appreciation of financial markets, and the huge uptick in the total wealth of our species, is never front-page news.

As a result, the majority of the population tends to have an extremely distorted view of financial markets, because the only time they ever hear about financial markets is when there has been a 'massive crash'.

This is another key reason why the majority of people don't invest. They think financial markets are fundamentally riskier and scarier than they actually are. Too many people think that the stock market is a 'casino' and believe that investing is basically gambling. This is entirely the wrong view to take about investment. It's down to a huge failure in our education and media systems. And it's incredibly damaging to many millions of people's chances of becoming wealthy.

Another important point to make here is that there is plenty of evidence that all of this is also really bad for our mental health. All over the world, and particularly in the developed world, rates of depression and mental illness are at historically high levels. This is the case despite the fact that most people today have far better lives, in terms of wealth and comfort at least, than most human beings who ever lived in history, as we saw earlier in this book.

This powerful negative bias in our press is one of the key drivers of mental illness, unhappiness and dissatisfaction. It is also one of the reasons all too many people spend so much time being angry and arguing with each other online.

To be clear, in making this case I don't want to appear too naive. There are of course real problems in the world, but it is pretty clear that many of these problems get blown out of all proportion, and get far too much focus overall as compared to anything positive. This has negative consequences for all of us.

In many ways, this is actually one of the biggest tragedies of our time. Happily, there is a solution, though: to educate yourself about the *true* state of the world, believe in human progress, and learn about financial markets so that you can maximize your chances of benefiting from that progress and of leading the best life you can.

If you do this, you have a much higher chance of being wealthy and, arguably even more importantly, fundamentally more happy along the way, too. There is a well-known saying in investment circles:

Pessimists sound smart, optimists make money.

You have to ask yourself: would you rather sound smart… or be rich?

Theme 2: Inflation – 'not one man in a million'

So the world economy is growing because of human progress. If you are an investor in that progress and growth, you are far more likely to become wealthy than people who aren't. As we saw a few pages back, however, at the same time that the world is growing, and in part as a consequence of that growth, there is quite a lot of a nasty thing called 'inflation' in many parts of the world. This is another topic that is important for you to understand given the impact it can and will have on your ability to become wealthy.

John Maynard Keynes was arguably the most famous economist of the 20th century. In 1919 he argued:

> By a continuing process of inflation, governments can confiscate, secretly and unobserved, an important part of the wealth of their citizens.

He went on to say that 'not one man in a million is able to diagnose' the impact of inflation. This was quite an extreme statement, given that it suggests that only a few thousand people in the whole world understand inflation properly out of more than eight billion of us, but he probably wasn't all that far off. Very few people understand inflation and the impact it can have on their wealth, particularly over many years.

You will probably know that inflation has been in the news quite a lot in recent years and has been a big political issue. This is because inflation makes us all poorer, so it is perhaps no surprise that people get angry and it becomes a political issue when it is high. As we shall see in this part of the book, however, it is actually even higher than most people understand. Governments like to keep it that way because people would be even angrier if they realized this was the case. Real inflation being higher than most people realize is one of the key reasons that many people feel poorer nowadays without really understanding why.

So what is inflation? At the most basic level, it is simply the increase in the price of the things we need or want to buy. If a loaf of bread cost \$1 last year, and it costs \$1.20 this year, then inflation in the price of a loaf of bread is 20%. These sorts of price increases have become quite common in recent years with things like pasta increasing in price anywhere from 30% in the US to as much as 90% in the UK. There have been big price rises in all sorts of everyday things, including olive oil, cheese and butter, but also in things that cost much more money, like cars, luxury goods, and healthcare.

If the price of the things you want to buy goes up by, say, 20%, but your income stays the same, this makes you 20% poorer. In real terms, this is no different to suffering a 20% pay cut!

Because of how important inflation is, and what a big impact it has on all of us, governments all over the world calculate various inflation numbers for the whole economy, so we can all have an idea of how much poorer we are getting each year, and, theoretically, so the government can do their best to keep it reasonably low. This is where the trouble starts. I would argue that many government inflation numbers are very misleading and don't really give people an accurate picture of the real increase in the cost of living. This is something that's very important to understand, even if very few people do.

The way governments all over the world calculate overall inflation in the economy is to choose a big, mixed basket of products and services that is supposed to be representative of the economy overall. They then compare the prices of those things from year to year. In the US, the calculation includes many thousands of things, and in the UK several hundred.

Because the government organizations that produce these numbers get to choose what goes into that basket, there is quite a lot they can do to deliver numbers that are more politically acceptable than what many people's real-life experience of inflation might actually be.

There are three things the government does to produce inflation numbers that are lower than the true increase in the cost of living for many people. This makes people think they are wealthier than they really are, and it also means that governments are able to pay out less money to their citizens when it comes to things like pensions and social security, because those payments are linked to the 'official' inflation numbers.

These three things are called 'substitution', 'weighting' and 'hedonic adjustment'. Although this might sound quite technical, this stuff is important enough for your future wealth that it is worth explaining them as best I can in plain English. Let's look at each in turn:

- *Substitution*: this is where the people who calculate inflation numbers replace something in the basket of goods that is getting more expensive with something else that isn't, or that may even have fallen in price. For example, they might replace fillet steak with minced beef, or wild salmon with farmed salmon. If they do this, even if steak and salmon have become a great deal more expensive, the inflation number won't budge. As you can imagine, this is quite an easy game to play when you get to choose what goes in the basket!
- *Weighting*: at the time of writing, the healthcare sector in the US is worth about 16% of the US economy, but healthcare products and services only make up about 6–8% of the basket used to calculate US inflation. This is also quite an easy game to play. If an area of the economy, like healthcare, is experiencing very high levels of inflation, as it has for many years, all you need to do to limit the effect this has on the overall inflation number is include fewer healthcare products and services in the basket.
- *Hedonic adjustment:* this is arguably the most complicated and 'sneaky' one of the three. Hedonic adjustment is when an item is reduced in price for the purposes of the inflation calculation because the authorities argue that you're getting more for your money and you are therefore *effectively* paying less. As an example, let's say that last year a 55-inch TV from Sony or Samsung cost 1,000 dollars or pounds. This year there is a new 55-inch TV that also costs 1,000 dollars or pounds, but that has a slightly better screen and picture, and a nicer remote control with more buttons on it. Although a very similar 55-inch TV costs the same, the people who calculate such things will argue that the TV is, say, 20% better than last year's TV and adjust its price in the inflation calculation from $1,000 down to $800. The TV still actually costs $1,000, but they have included it in the calculation at $800. This trick is used to adjust the price of lots of products that go into the inflation calculation.

When they find out about this stuff, lots of people think that this is some kind of conspiracy, but this really isn't the case. I'm not making any of this up, and this isn't a conspiracy theory. All the information I'm sharing in this section of the book is widely available online, but very few people in the general population understand this stuff. Even some people who work in the media, or in banking and finance, don't get it. You are now in the tiny minority of people who do, which should give you a big advantage in the years ahead!

Hidden inflation

There are other ways the official inflation numbers can underestimate the actual increase in your cost of living. One source of 'hidden inflation' that doesn't make it into the official numbers is sometimes called 'ghostflation' or 'shrinkflation'. This is where a company gives you less of something for the same price 'on the sly', something that has been happening a great deal in recent years.

Examples include the fact that cereal boxes have been reduced in size by more than 20% in the last few years, with no change in price. This has also happened with numerous well-known brands of chocolate, potato chips, frozen snacks and ice cream. Toilet rolls have fewer sheets in them. Boxes of laundry detergent have shrunk, too. If you start paying attention to these sorts of things, you realize that examples can be found in pretty much every aisle of the supermarket.

To be fair to the companies doing this, the main reason they have needed to is because their costs are going up, too. They are experiencing their own inflation. If the cost of things like wheat, cocoa and energy is going up, companies need to pass those costs on to their customers so that they can remain profitable. Rather than raise prices, one of the easiest ways to do this is to give you less for the same money in the hope that you won't notice!

Inflation is 'zero' but so many things are at all-time highs

The other thing that should make us a bit suspicious when governments tell us that inflation numbers are 'low', is the fact that, all over the world, the prices of many financial assets are at or near all-time highs. This has been true for some years as lots and lots of things just keep getting more and more expensive, year after year.

At the time of writing, there is a long list of places in the world where house prices are at or near the highest they have ever been in history. This includes places like London, Sydney, Melbourne, Dubai, Singapore, Tokyo, Vancouver, Toronto, New York, Miami and so on; the list is long.

The same is true of *stock markets* in many parts of the world. The main US stock market, the S&P 500 (which we will look at in more detail soon), is close to all-time highs, as are stock markets in Japan, Australia, Singapore, Germany, France, Switzerland, Denmark and Sweden. This is the case even though Europe isn't doing all that well economically or politically at the moment.

The same has been true of fine wine, rare spirits such as whiskey and brandy, and vintage cars. These things are all also at or near all-time highs. So are gold and bitcoin, two other important financial assets.

How can governments all over the world keep telling us that inflation is 'low' when the increase in the prices of so many things is not?

The price of nearly all of the things you actually need in your life – food, fuel, shelter, medical care, insurance, education and so on – has been going up a lot for many years, and much more quickly than is suggested by the 'official' numbers. This means that, unless your wealth or your income is going up by at least as much, you are getting poorer.

What causes inflation? Why is this happening?

Milton Friedman is another very famous economist who won the Nobel Prize in Economics in 1976. One of his most famous quotes was about inflation:

> Inflation is always and everywhere a monetary phenomenon.

Although this sounds a bit complicated, his point was just that inflation comes as a result of there being too much money. This might sound a bit odd, but let's try and explain what he meant because this is really important.

Imagine there is a fixed supply of actual, tangible 'stuff' in the world, such as crops, metals, oil, concrete, clothes, cars and so on.

Imagine, too, there is x amount of money, whether dollars, pounds, euros, yen or whatever else.

Now imagine if governments all over the world simply decide to wave a magic wand and double the amount of money in the world overnight. Crucially, if they do this, there won't be any more 'stuff' the following day. Farmers won't have had time to grow any more crops. Oil companies won't have been able to produce any more oil. Factories won't have made any more clothes, TVs, cars and so on.

If there is twice as much money and the same amount of stuff, then all that happens is the price of stuff will double. If there is twice as much money chasing the same quantity of goods and services, those goods and services will double in price, all other things being equal.

It isn't quite as simple as that in real life, but this is basically what happens. If there is twice as much money, someone has that money, and they are therefore able to pay more for the stuff they want, which means prices go up. We have centuries of evidence for this real-world outcome. This is a very important concept to understand and all too few people do, including most of our politicians nowadays (seemingly) and more than a few economics professors!

Stuff is real wealth; money is not. Money is just a technology or tool that we use as a medium of exchange and a store of value, as we saw earlier.

The reason that real inflation, the real cost of living, and so many asset prices have been going up is because governments all over the world have been creating huge amounts of money for many decades now, essentially out of thin air. We use the word 'creating' rather than 'printing' because very little of this new money is actually printed as notes or minted as coins; it is simply 'invented' in computers. This creates inflation. We will look at this reality in more detail later in the book when we cover a financial asset class called 'bonds'.

What this means for you

Remember that when there is high inflation, you are getting poorer, unless your income or wealth is increasing by at least as much as the rate of inflation. When there is significant inflation, the value of cash falls as the price of 'things' increases.

The best way to deal with this is to make sure you own the things that are going up in price. As we have just seen, this will include many financial assets such as shares, gold and property. We don't need to understand in detail why stock markets, gold, oil, wheat, cotton, coffee, art, houses, jewellery and wine go up in price when there is inflation. It is enough just to be aware that this is the case, so that you have the best chance of doing something about it and doing your best to avoid becoming poorer as a result!

Now that you understand inflation and how the global economy continues to grow, you are better placed than the vast majority of people because you can take advantage of that understanding.

In the next section of the book, we will look at what to do to benefit from the two facts about finance and our two crucial themes we have just covered in this section.

Before we do, it's worth summarizing what we have learned so far:

- Money is not 'the root of all evil'. Money and financial markets are just a technology which have helped our species enormously since they were invented.
- To do good you must first do well. If you want to help people, it helps to be rich.
- It has never been more important to understand what is happening in finance, if you want to maximize the chance you become wealthy and minimize the risk you become (or stay) poor.
- It isn't as hard to do this as you might think. You are probably only a few hours away from making a huge difference.
- You need to ensure you benefit from the incredible power of compound interest.
- Financial products today are better than ever before – if you know where to find the best ones at the right price.
- The world economy is growing and will continue to grow thanks to human progress, 'the most important investment theme in history'. You need to 'own the world'.
- There is significant real inflation in the world. You need to 'own inflation'.

PART II

Finance basics – what you need to know

- Finding the money:
  - Budgeting
  - The role of property
- First things first:
  - Pay off any expensive debt
  - Build up a 'rainy day' pot of cash
- The key asset classes:
  - Cash
  - Property (or real estate)
  - Bonds
  - Shares (otherwise known as 'stocks' or 'equities')
  - Commodities
  - Funds
  - Currencies (or foreign exchange)
  - Crypto
- The key accounts you will need:
  - A 'checking', 'current', 'transaction' or 'everyday' account
  - A pension account of some kind
  - An investment account of some kind

5

Finding the money / ‘creating financial surplus’

As we saw in the first part of this book, the highest probability way that you will become wealthy is by becoming an *investor*. In these next two sections, we are going to look at the nuts and bolts of how to do that.

We will look at what you need to do to find the money to start investing. We'll also discuss the different investment products and financial assets you will want to understand and use to build wealth.

So, let's start with a fairly important topic first: how to find the money to invest! It should be clear from what you have read so far that if you want to be wealthy – if you want to have real financial security, the finer things in life, and have the power to do more good, too – you should live by a very simple formula that is well understood by the rich and that has remained unchanged for the several thousand years since humans invented money:

Live on less than you earn and invest the rest!

Earlier in the book, we saw just how powerful compounding is. Even if you do not have much money to invest, do not let this put you off! It is best to start saving *something* as soon as you can, and then let compound interest and time work their magic. Even very small amounts of money saved and invested now can and will make a big difference to your life in the future, particularly if you are lucky enough to start on this road when you are quite young.

If you want to win at the money game, it is really important to make sure that you free up at least *some* spare money in your life. This is also something you should aim to do forever. Investing is not something you do for a little while and then stop. It should be a 'non-negotiable' life habit that you decide to do, and continue to do every month, from the minute you earn any money, until the time you have built meaningful – hopefully life-changing – wealth.

So, let's first turn our attention to how you are going to find some financial surplus – that is, some spare money to invest.

Making / earning money

As its title suggests, this book is aimed at an audience that has a very wide range of incomes. For younger readers, if you are still at college or university, you may not be earning anything at all yet. If you are in your late twenties and have a great job, you might already be a high earner. Wherever you are on that journey, however, a key point to make is that it is important to make earning, saving and investing a priority as soon as you can. It is key to think this way, big picture, because it increases the chances that you will get things sorted, and make the most of the huge time advantage you have as a younger adult.

My experience as a teenager and then as a university student might be instructive here. From a young age, I did a paper round in Wimbledon[1] in south-west London, where I grew up, and was paid the princely sum of £15 a week (for seven days a week of getting up very early!). This doesn't sound like much, but this was in the 1980s and I was able to earn as much as 12% a year on those savings in a UK savings account. I was also lucky enough to sing on the soundtrack of a couple of Hollywood movies in my early teens and used to be paid for singing at weddings and funerals too. I also worked quite a few shifts in a bar the year before I went to university.

All of that added up. I had several thousand pounds when I went to university in 1994, quite a big chunk of which I had earned as interest, given how high interest rates were in the late 1980s (the power of compounding!).

Once at university, I continued to sing and work in various bars, both during term time and over the holidays. What this meant was that I was able to leave university with relatively little debt overall. Sadly, things have changed since then in the UK, and university is far more expensive now, as it is in the US.

This does not change the general point here, however, which is that it is a good idea to try and earn at least *some* money as soon as you can in life. If you keep an open mind, there will often be things you can do to make this happen.

It is generally not possible for a teenager, or someone in their early twenties who's still at university, to get a full-time job, not least given the time needed for study and plenty of extra-curricular activities like sport or music. That said, more often than not, it *is* possible to

---

[1] Of tennis fame for any of you who are tennis fans!

get a part-time job to get at least some money coming in, whether that might be in a local restaurant, hotel, coffee shop, cinema, theatre, sports club, supermarket, pub or bar. Other ideas include things like tutoring, babysitting, dog walking and lots else besides.

The chances are that you can find a job with flexible hours before or after school, college or university, or on the weekends, and work a few hours a week to earn some extra cash.

Of course, nowadays, the internet and social media can provide you with ways of making money, and help you find the jobs listed above too. None of this was available to me in the 1980s. A lot of the stuff that's out there now is far easier, more powerful and more lucrative than paper rounds or working in a bar! If you have something you're passionate about, it is entirely possible to make money on platforms like YouTube, Tik Tok and Instagram if you're willing to put the work in, and there are a wealth of online resources that can teach you how to do that, many of which are free of charge.

Here's an (admittedly extreme) example of what's possible. In 2013, a 17-year-old British student called Nick D'Aloisio managed to sell his news app Summly to Yahoo for more than £20 million. There are plenty of other examples, including many online influencers who have made a great deal of money starting from a young age. Of course, then there are the musicians who started making money in their teens, including folks like Justin Bieber, Billie Eilish and Shawn Mendes in the US; Adele and Joss Stone in the UK; and Lorde in New Zealand. Many of the world's highest-paid actors and actresses also started in their teens, or even earlier than that, including Leonardo DiCaprio, Jennifer Lawrence, Timothée Chalamet, Tom Holland, Zendaya, and dozens of others.

It might seem a bit ridiculous to use enormously successful global celebrities as examples of what is possible, but the key point is that nowadays the internet can enable anyone from anywhere to make at least some money. You may not go on to be a massive global star or a multi-millionaire influencer, but it might be easier than you think to make at least a few hundred or even a few thousand dollars or pounds a month. The most important thing to understand about all of this, however, is that it does take a long time and a lot of work to get to a point where you will consistently make money. More often than not you will need several years to get there.

Unless you are very lucky, the nature of growing any kind of business on the internet is that not much happens for a long time. You have to be very consistent and keep going, often for much longer than many people are willing to. As leading online entrepreneur Alex Hormozi has put it:

> The world belongs to those who can keep doing without seeing the result of their doing.[2]

This is another example of why compounding is such an important idea to understand, when it comes to nearly everything. If you double your audience every few months, it might not feel like you're making much progress for a long time, at least in terms of your ability to make money. But several years into that process your online audience will suddenly explode, and you will finally be rewarded for all that time and effort and consistency.

As leading podcaster Chris Williamson has explained about his Modern Wisdom channel:

> It took us 5 years, 600 episodes and 1000 videos to hit 1 million. It's taken 9 months and 120 episodes to hit 2 million. We gained more subscribers in the last month than the entire first 3 years of the show.[3]

Less than a year after he made this comment he is now at more than 3 million! The key point is that when he was several hundred videos into that journey, he probably wasn't making that much money, even after three years! When it comes to doing anything online the 'secret' is to keep going long past the time when most people give up. This is actually true of many things in life more generally, including investment. This is another advantage that young people have and another great example of the power of compounding.

---

[2] Alex Hormozi (@AlexHormozi), 'The world belongs to those who can keep doing without seeing the result of their doing', X (formerly Twitter), 17 July 2022, 3:50 AM, https://x.com/AlexHormozi/status/1548500270534967296?lang=en

[3] Chris Williamson (Chris Willx). YouTube Community Post. 2024. https://www.youtube.com/post/Ugkx5KDUWl-p5WBMjeQq6tBXXbzuMRGLU4WQ

The other thing that is possible nowadays that wasn't when I was growing up is the ability to sell things online. Nowadays there are a large number of online marketplaces that make it easier than ever to sell things. Arguably the best-known of these are eBay and Facebook Marketplace. In the US there is also Craigslist and in the UK there's Gumtree. Then there are fashion-focused apps like Depop and Vinted, and sites where you can sell things you have made like Etsy and Not On The High Street.

All of this makes it easier to make at least *some* money nowadays – another big advantage you have over previous generations. Of course, if you already have a job, all of this could be some way easier, and you won't have to think about selling things online, although you could do both, to maximize money coming in!

Budgeting

So, assuming now that you have at least some money coming in, the next thing is to work out how to ensure some of that money goes towards saving and investing.

Three broad approaches

There's lots of advice flying around online about the 'best' approach when it comes to finding the money for saving and investment. Over the years, I've seen all sorts of weird and wonderful ideas. Some of them are helpful and others are extreme enough to make life pretty miserable.

Distilling down a lot of this thinking, perhaps the three most common approaches which make sense and can help you get the right mix of saving and enjoying life, too, are the following ones:

THE 90/10 APPROACH

This is the easiest one: the idea is that, whatever you do, you should ensure that you save and invest at least 10% of whatever you earn without fail. As soon as you start to earn money, make sure that you are able to live on 90% of that money and put 10% of it by for saving and investment. This is certainly a good place to start.

THE 50/30/20 APPROACH

Next up is an idea that has become particularly popular in recent years. You'll find it all over the internet if you go looking for such things. The 50/30/20 idea is that you should divide your income into three categories: 'needs', 'wants' and 'savings'. Here is how it works:

1. 50% of what you earn should be spent on your 'needs' – that is, essential expenses that you *have* to spend money on. This would include:
   a. Your home – i.e. rent or mortgage payments
   b. Your utility bills – energy, phone, internet, etc.
   c. Groceries
   d. Any insurance you need to have – medical, property, car, phone and so on
   e. Transportation costs that you cannot avoid – fuel, bus fare, etc.
2. 30% of your money can then go towards your 'wants' – in other words, non-essential things that you would *like* to spend money on. This would include:
   a. Going out to restaurants or concerts
   b. Sports and hobbies like gaming
   c. Subscription services like Netflix, Apple TV, Spotify and so on
   d. Non-essential clothing or electronic equipment such as TVs or gaming consoles
   e. Holidays.
3. 20% of your income is then left over for saving and investment. This money should go towards:
   a. Building an emergency or 'rainy day' fund of cash (more on that shortly)
   b. Paying down any debt you have, ideally until you have none at all (more on this shortly too)
   c. Saving for key long-term goals and big expenses, such as a home, car, or wedding
   d. Investing for your retirement – generally called your 'pension'
   e. Other investments like shares or other assets (which we will cover later in this section of the book).

50/30/20 is a sensible way of looking at the world, and should do a good job at taking care of your immediate needs and wants. It also increases the chances of you becoming wealthy over time.

The 33/33/33 approach

The last of the three approaches is very similar to 50/30/20, just with a different split. 33/33/33 suggests that you should spend one third of your money on 'living expenses', another third on 'enjoyment', and then keep the remaining third aside for saving and investment. These are essentially the same categories we just covered.

This idea is generally attributed to an American writer named George S. Clason. He published a book called *The Richest Man in Babylon* in 1926. It's still in print today nearly a century later, and is one of the best-selling personal finance books of all time. That book popularized the idea of 33/33/33.

Perhaps a key point to make about 33/33/33 is that it comes from a very different era. The main difference between then and now is the price of property. As we shall see shortly when we look at property in a bit more detail, one way to think about the cost of property is to consider how many times the average wage an average property costs.

If the average person earns about £40,000 a year and an average property costs £160,000, this is four times the average wage. If the average property costs £400,000, this is ten times.

In the 1920s, when Clason wrote his book, the price of an average property in the US was only about three to five times the average annual income. In the UK it was more like two to three times the average annual income, particularly throughout the 1930s, when Britain built a lot of new houses.

Nowadays houses and apartments are much more expensive. The average property in the US today is about seven and a half times the average salary[4] and more than eight times in the UK![5] In cities

[4] https://www.visualcapitalist.com/median-house-prices-vs-income-us/

[5] https://www.ons.gov.uk/peoplepopulationandcommunity/housing/bulletins/housingaffordabilityinenglandandwales/2023

like London and New York, these multiples are even higher at more like ten or even 12 times!

This is the main reason why the idea of 33/33/33 has evolved towards 50/30/20 over the course of the last few decades. Since the cost of putting a roof over our heads is much higher today than it was a century ago, we have to spend rather more on our 'needs' than we did in the past. If you are lucky enough to be a high earner, however, the 33/33/33 ratio is still possible to maintain, and it becomes even more so as you get older, if you keep control of your expenses as you (hopefully) earn more.

The FIRE movement

Before we move on, there is one more idea I should at least mention in passing: the FIRE movement. FIRE stands for 'Financial Independence Retire Early' and has become very popular in recent years. The idea of FIRE is to make saving and investing a very high priority in your life, with the aim of achieving financial independence and being able to 'retire' many years before traditional retirement age. It is particularly popular with people who work in the tech sector who can be paid very well at a young age and often know quite a lot about money and financial markets.

If you are lucky enough to be paid very well, keep your costs low, make investment a big priority in your life, and do a solid job when you invest, it is possible to get to a point where you have enough money to live on for the rest of your life at quite a young age. One of the reasons people who work in tech and similar jobs for which basically all you need is an internet connection can do this is because they can choose to live in lower-cost cities and towns, or even lower-cost countries. This can significantly reduce what they spend on property and also on commuting and travel. Living in a very expensive city and having to travel into and out of it every day can eat up a huge amount of your income, even if you are a high earner.

People in the FIRE movement look to save as much of their income as they possibly can. This can range from about 25% all the way up to as much as 70% for people who are particularly high earners or willing to cut their expenses to the bone. Their ultimate goal is to build up an investment portfolio that is about 25 times what they need to live on each year. This is because, if you assume that you can reliably earn at least 4% a year on your investments, which is certainly a realistic goal as we shall see later in the book, you will be able to live on that investment return.

To keep the maths easy, if you had £1 million, you should be able to pay yourself at least £40,000 a year forever! This is an exciting position to be in, as I hope you'll agree.

Many people think the idea of getting to this sort of six- or even seven-figure amount is unrealistic. As we've already shown, however, because of the power of compounding, this is not the case. Even people on average incomes can realistically aspire to achieve this if they do a good job with investment over a long enough period of time. The problem is that too few people understand compounding, and even fewer take advantage of it!

A final point to make here about budgeting, before we move on, is the fact that there are certain things you might want to spend money on for which it might not be clear which category of the 50/30/20 distribution they fall into. This is especially true of things that cost you a lot of money. Should a holiday, car or wedding come out of your 30% of 'wants' money or out of the 20% you're saving and investing?

There is no hard and fast rule here. If you are lucky enough to land a high-paying job, you may be able to pay for such things without having to save up for them, especially if you're happy with cheaper holidays and cars.

Of course, there *will* be things that you will want to save up for over a period of time. It is important to stress that this is always a much better approach than using credit card or other debt to buy such things.

The other very important point to make is that, whatever you decide to do about these sorts of purchases, you should do your very best to save *something* every month.

In many parts of the world, if you have a job, you should get a pension of some kind from your employer. It is likely that you will also be contributing to a government pension scheme if you are working.

One way to think about 50/30/20 then, is that you spend 50% on needs and 30% on fun, or 'wants'. Then you split the 20% left over for saving and investing into two halves (of 10% each), as follows:

- 10% should be what you save for retirement. This is *something you do forever without fail and never touch until you retire.* For many people this will be covered in their pension arrangements, both from their employer, and likely from the government too in some shape or form.
- Another 10% should then be invested on top of that, to build wealth faster and also to save towards those big expenses like a car, holiday, wedding or deposit on a property. This is actually the 10% we looked at in the 90/10 rule above – because the 90/10 approach assumes you've already got a pension. Hopefully this all makes sense!

In conclusion, if at all possible you want to arrange things so that you invest or save *at least* 10% of any money you earn, without fail, no matter what is going on with your life. You will want to do this from the moment you start making any money at all, and keep doing it until the time that you reach the goal of being able to live on your money, not your work. The better a job you do, the sooner this can happen. Happily, in many parts of the world, and particularly the developed world, this 10% will very often be covered by your pension arrangements.

Crucially, however, you should then do your best to find *another* 10% to invest, over and above your pension. This will help you get to that goal more quickly and will also help you afford the more expensive things you might want to buy along the way.

One of the tragedies of the modern age is how few people do this. Far too many people convince themselves that they're just not able to find any money. They don't do anything about this year after year. In the end, this is a huge part of the reason so many people struggle financially in their lives. The good news is that it really isn't as hard as it seems. It just requires a bit of planning and thought.

Reframing

One trick that can help you when you try to work out how to find the money to start saving and investing is to flip the whole idea of 'budgeting' and 'saving' on its head. Instead of trying to work out how on earth you're going to *save* 10% of your income, work out how you would most enjoy *spending* 90% of it!

This might sound a bit strange and is obviously just a case of 'glass half full versus glass half empty', but the weird thing is that it actually works. Thinking carefully about what you'd like to *spend* 90% of your money on is much more fun than working out how to save money.

If you say to yourself 'I am going to spend 90% of my money on x, y and z', and then *automate* what happens with the remaining 10%, you are likely to find it easier than you thought to have 10% of your income available for saving and investment.

Psychologists describe this kind of thing as 'reframing'. There is lots of evidence that reframing can be a very powerful technique for change in any area of your life. The idea that you might think in some detail about how to *spend* your money, is sometimes called 'mindful', 'conscious' or 'intentional' spending.

At the risk of sounding a bit 'woo-woo' or new-age, this approach uses an 'abundance' rather than a 'scarcity' mindset. Interestingly, many years of psychological research indicates that adopting an abundance mindset tends to make us happier. The evidence shows that when we focus on what we have, rather than what we lack, we tend to experience higher levels of satisfaction in our lives. It also increases the chance that we become wealthy over time.

Thinking about all the lovely ways you might *spend* as much as 90% of your money every month does just this, and can actually be a pretty exciting and fun exercise when you think about it. By giving real focus to what you're going to buy, you do a much better job at being thoughtful about your purchases. You develop a proper plan and stop yourself from spending money on pointless stuff that you don't really need or want. Doing this has a really good chance of freeing up that money to save and invest, and can feel far less restrictive and annoying than focusing on how to save.

Start small, but do start!

Perhaps the most important point to make overall is how important it is to *get started*, even if you are only able to save and invest a very small amount of money. Nowadays, many investment platforms and financial apps let you invest tiny amounts of money. This is absolutely worth doing, for three key reasons:

- First, because of the incredible power of compounding. If you do start small, no matter how small, you will enable yourself to benefit from the magic of compound interest as you go through your life. As we have already seen, over long periods of time very small amounts of money can become much larger amounts!
- Second, and perhaps more importantly, the evidence is that if you do manage to do this, and build a regular, automated saving and investment habit, you are then more than likely to save and invest more over time, particularly as you see the results you can achieve.
- Third, if you do this, you are also far more likely to learn a great deal more about money and investment over time than if you don't. There is nothing like having some money actually on the line to increase your interest in the topic and the amount of time you spend focused on it and thinking about it. This is likely to be a very good thing.

Just getting started will more than likely nudge you onto a completely different trajectory in your life. You might only start with a very small number of dollars or pounds to begin with, but once you've set this up as a key life habit, you are then much more likely to increase those numbers over time. This is likely to be life-changing. You will have a solid chance of becoming wealthy over time.

People who never start at all have a much lower probability of getting this result. With money, as with so many things in life, like exercise, studying or reading, it is the tortoise who generally wins the race, not the hare. 'Little and often' is the way to go with most things that really matter.

You are much more likely to save a small amount of money right now than you are to save a large amount of money sometime in the distant future. You also get a huge benefit the sooner you start. Time is one of your biggest allies for building wealth, as we have seen. Building wealth is a marathon, not a sprint.

Far too few people do this. One of the main reasons people don't is because they think they need a large amount of money to make it all worthwhile. Too many people think investment is 'for rich people'. As we've seen, this is an incorrect and incredibly limiting belief. It's one of the key reasons so many people don't invest, and struggle financially as a result.

If you want to become wealthy, you need to build up your saving and investing 'muscles'. This is no different from the idea that if you want to be fit and healthy, you need to build up your actual muscles through regular exercise.

The key thing is to find even a small amount of money for saving and investment as soon as you can, and get started. Don't ever think that doing so is a waste of time.

If you've only just started working, and you're not earning that much, you will only have a small amount to invest. Another key point that is worth dwelling on, however, is the fact that many people earn more money as they get older. At the risk of stating the obvious, it will be easier to save and invest the more you earn. Within reason, many of life's costs can be relatively fixed. As you get older and earn more, if you keep a lid on 'lifestyle creep', you will find it increasingly easy to find at least 10% or even more of what you earn for saving and investment.

Many people gradually earn more money as they get older. If you've already built some kind of automated investing *habit* in your twenties or thirties, it is so much easier to gradually increase the amount you save and invest as you go. Again, this will very likely deliver a life-changing result over time.

In our next chapter we will turn our attention to property. Putting a roof over your head is usually your biggest expense in life, so it's important for us to look at it in some detail.

6
The crucial role played by property (when it comes to finding the money)

As we saw a few pages back, property has become a particularly big expense in recent decades. Nowadays, it tends to cost us all far more than it did in the past in many parts of the world. As a result, more than ever, the choices you make about where you live, and whether you rent or try to buy a property, will be really important for whether or not you can build wealth.

This is another advantage that many young people have nowadays. Research shows that about one in three American adults aged between 18 and 34 live with their parents. These numbers are similar in the UK, and even higher in many European and Asian countries.[1]

Whilst many young adults may wish they could move out and find their own place, if you are living with your parents and they're willing to let you live with them for free, or charge you less rent than a private landlord would, this could at least mean you are in a position to save and invest quite a lot more than someone who has taken the decision to move out.

If you are in this situation, the better a job you do with saving and investing, the sooner you will be able to find your own place and move out! It is really important to stress, however, that when you do make that decision, getting what you spend on property right is very important. Another reason that lots of people struggle financially is because they make bad choices when it comes to where they live and whether to rent or buy. Given how important a topic this is, it is worth looking at it in a little detail before we move on.

It isn't that controversial to say that there is something of an obsession with property ownership, particularly in English-speaking countries like the US, UK and Australia. There is a great deal of pressure from society as a whole to 'get on the property ladder'. This can actually get people into real trouble financially, and has also been one of the causes of a number of financial crises in recent decades, particularly the 'sub-prime' 'global financial crisis' of 2007–9.

Although you may be some years away from being in a position to buy a property, it is still important to understand the relative merits of buying as compared to renting. Relatively few people

---

[1] https://www.pewresearch.org/short-reads/2023/05/03/in-the-u-s-and-abroad-more-young-adults-are-living-with-their-parents/

have a really detailed understanding of such things, including many realtors and estate agents. The good news is that understanding this issue in a little more detail could also make you more relaxed about being a renter. Many young adults feel a great deal of pressure to figure out how to buy a property, often far sooner than is a good idea for them.

We have lived through many years of people saying things like 'you can't go wrong with bricks and mortar'; 'rent is throwing money away'; or you're 'paying someone else's mortgage' when you rent.

Contrary to what well-meaning relatives might have you believe, many of these statements are overly simplistic and often entirely incorrect. Like all financial assets, property is sometimes good value, and sometimes it is dangerously expensive and it can be a very bad decision to buy it, particularly if you stretch yourself financially to do so.

In plenty of times and places throughout history, there has actually been more of a 'property snake' than a property ladder. The problem is that all too few people look at a long enough period of history when they think about property, or understand in any detail the various 'fundamental' ways you might value it.

Many very rich people understand this stuff. Billionaire Jim Rogers, arguably one of the best investors of all time, has twice sold all his property on the eve of a crash (in 1987 and 2007). He regularly describes property as a fundamentally bad investment because of how hard and expensive it is to buy and sell, and because of the large number of costs involved in owning it.

There are plenty of other examples of extremely wealthy and successful people who have a similar view of property. You might find this surprising given how unusual it is to hold any kind of negative view of property ownership, particularly in the English-speaking world.

Given the huge difference it can make to your finances, it is worth taking a closer look at property and how to value it. The decisions you make about property in particular will have a huge impact on your wealth over your lifetime – and the wrong decision can potentially damage your financial situation for decades. As ever, the money game is a marathon, not a sprint. This fact should be borne in mind when making any decision as big as buying a property.

Most people in the English-speaking world are familiar with property as an asset class. There is a long tradition of people wanting to own their own homes in places like the US, UK and Australia, but this is less the case in many other countries in the world, including in wealthy European nations like Germany and France, where a high percentage of the population rent, often for their entire lives.

House prices are a national obsession in the US, UK and Australia, and are regularly discussed in the press. Property tends to be an individual's biggest financial asset and there is also an understandable emotional attachment to your home over and above the attachment you might have to a share or any other type of investment. You can't live in a share certificate or a bar of gold!

The problem with this is that many people feel that they are 'experts' when it comes to property, and never more so than in the last few decades. Because property prices have gone up a lot for many years and in many places, all too many people assume that this is what always happens.

Anchoring

This is something that psychologists call 'anchoring'. If something has been true in your personal experience – property prices have gone up – you will tend to assume that this is what always happens. All too often, we believe that something that has been true during our lifetime, or even for a few years, will continue to be true forever.

But this is often not the case and it can get people into real trouble, particularly when it comes to financial assets like property, which can definitely go down in value. To get a more accurate picture of things, it is a good idea to consider much longer timeframes. This can be challenging as the information is more difficult to find. You generally won't see the press talking about home prices over the course of many decades. Nevertheless, it is possible to find that kind of evidence and it is absolutely worth doing.

And it is worth highlighting that, in the very long run, looking at more than 300 years of data, property is absolutely not the 'sure thing' most people have come to believe it is. The idea that 'you can't go wrong with bricks and mortar' can be a dangerous one!

Key metrics / the key things you need to know

As we shall see later in the book, when you look at any financial asset, it is important to understand certain 'key metrics' that can help you understand whether or not now is a good time to invest. The same is true when it comes to property. Far too few people really understand such things, including lots of supposed property professionals.

There isn't necessarily a magic formula to predict precisely whether now is a good or bad time to buy property, but there are certain metrics and methods for giving us a fighting chance of figuring out whether we are closer to a strong period for housing or a weak one, or whether a property you are looking at might be good value or not, just as there are for every other type of investment we are going to look at.

Because property will very likely be your biggest investment, and given how your choices in this area will affect your monthly cash flow and your ability to invest in anything else, it is important to understand these key measures of value before making any big decisions. Strangely, relatively few people do this. This is one of the reasons there are often property bubbles followed by big crashes.

So let us look at the key metrics we might use to understand real value in the property market. Like everything else you will find in this book, these really aren't that complicated. The tools used by smart professional investors are simple enough, and we should all have learned about them at school. The reality is, however, that they tend to be poorly understood by many people.

Inflation and property

First of all, it's important to think about inflation again. We looked at how important inflation is earlier in the book. It is particularly relevant when thinking about property, in the main because we tend to own properties for long periods of time. The longer you own something, the more of an impact inflation will have.

When it comes to inflation, economists and psychologists talk about something called 'money illusion'. This is the idea that many people don't think about inflation enough or even at all when they think of the value of something. This is particularly the case with property.

The real value of the dollar and the pound has fallen in value by more than 90% since the early 1970s. This is one of the main reasons why property prices from 50 years ago seem incredibly 'cheap' to us.

It was possible to buy a house or apartment back then for as little as $10,000, even in expensive cities like New York or London. Today, that same property would more than likely cost $500,000 or more. The *prices* are up as much as 50 times! Crucially, however, does this mean that the 'lucky' person who bought a house or apartment in the early 1970s has increased their *wealth* 50 times?

This is a pretty simple calculation, so you might assume that they have. Their property is up from $10,000 to $500,000, so they have 'made' 50 times their money. But you need to take account of inflation to understand whether they have grown their wealth in *real* terms.

The difference between wealth and money

Here we must look at one of the most important concepts in this book: the difference between wealth and money (particularly 'paper' money). In the example above, if the person sold their property they *would* certainly take away 50 times the amount of paper money (or currency) that they started with. They've grown their money by a factor of 50. Great news – at first glance, at least.

But what has happened to their real wealth? The key thing here is to look at how much the price of everything else has gone up by in the same time period (inflation!). The first and most obvious thing to look at is how much the price of other properties has increased. If this lucky person decides to sell their property, cash in their 'gains' but then buy another property in the same area, have they increased their wealth in terms of properties in the area?

The answer is obviously 'no'. If you sell a property and then buy another one in the same place, then the prices in that market will generally have gone up just as much as the price of your property.

So, even though this person has 50 times the amount of money that they had before, they can still only buy one relatively nice property in the same neighbourhood. Another similar property in the same area will cost exactly the same as the one they are selling.

Their real or true wealth – at least in terms of the property they own – has actually not increased at all.

Relative value

Now, imagine that the property in the example given above is in an expensive place like New York or London. Let's assume that when this person sells that property, they are doing so because they want to move to somewhere far less expensive. Perhaps they want to move from Manhattan to upstate New York or from London to Scotland.

It is quite possible that prices in those places might only have gone up half as much over the same time period. If this is the case, our lucky seller *has* increased their wealth in terms of the new property they want to buy in a cheaper property market. They can now buy twice as much property in upstate New York or Scotland than they could have done originally.

Their wealth in terms of upstate New York or Scottish properties has in fact doubled. This is obviously good news (assuming they want to move to those areas, of course). This shows that we should always be thinking about the *relative value* of things when trying to figure out if we are growing our wealth in real terms.

To expand on this example, let us say the price of a decent meal out for two in London cost £10 in the early 1970s. Today that same meal costs more like £200. Meals out are perhaps 20 times more expensive. This means that the property owner who sold their London flat is two and a half times better off in terms of meals out, because their property is up 50 times and meals out are only up 20 times (50/20 = 2.5).

Similarly, a flight from New York to London in the early 1970s might have cost about $200. To keep the arithmetic simple, let us say that the price today is around $2,000. In this example, our property owner who sold their New York apartment is five times richer in terms of flights from New York to London than they were in the early 1970s. Their property is up by 50 times; flights are up by ten times. This is because there has been far greater inflation in property prices than in the cost of air travel.

The point here is that if you want to build wealth you must always be thinking about comparative or relative value, and something called 'purchasing power' – basically what your money can actually buy you. A simple number in dollars or pounds actually tells you relatively little about whether you are truly getting richer or not.

This is true over shorter time frames than 50 or more years too. If your property is worth the same in dollars or pounds today as it was a few years ago but nearly everything you need to buy in your life (fuel, electricity, bread, eggs, milk, cars, train fares, insurance, healthcare) has gone up in price by 20–50%, as has been the case in recent years, then in real terms you are actually 20–50% poorer than you were a few years ago.

We can see just how important inflation is when considering the *true* value of property. There are two other key valuation metrics that we must be aware of to give us the best chance of working out whether properties are cheap or expensive: something called 'rental yield' and also the ratio of property prices to salaries.

Rental yield

One of the most useful ways of trying to work out if a property is truly cheap or expensive is the percentage return it would generate for you if you were to rent it out to someone. This is called the 'rental yield'.

Working out rental yield is a pretty simple calculation, but one that surprisingly few people make when considering the purchase of a property! I have met realtors who have never even heard of the idea, which is a bit like a doctor never having heard of a heart. Is it any wonder that, with 'professionals' like this, we so often suffer property price bubbles and the crashes that then follow?

Rental yield is the number you get if you divide the assumed annual rental income from a property by the assumed value of that property. It is a number that you can then use to compare the returns on property to any other asset you might be thinking about, including shares or other properties. It can also give you an idea of whether a property is cheap or expensive at a fundamental level. High rental yields suggest that it might be cheap; low rental yields that it could be expensive.

Let us assume you owned the £500,000 property we discussed in the examples above. Then assume that you are able to rent it out for £2,000 a month. This means that you will make £24,000 per year on that property. This is called the 'gross' rental income. Expressed as a 'yield' we would say that this property is generating 4.8% of gross rental yield for its owner (£24,000 / £500,000 = 4.8%).

Bear in mind, however, that as a landlord you will usually have to spend a certain amount each year on the maintenance of a property and on fixtures and fittings. There is also a chance that your property will lie void (be empty) from time to time if you can't immediately find a tenant to replace one who has left. Both of these things will have a negative impact on your rental income.

If you were sensible, you might assume that a rental property will be void one month a year on average over time, and that annual expenditure on maintenance, fixtures and fittings will total another 10% of the gross rental income.

Continuing with the example above, this means that the 'net' rental income from the property is likely to be more like £19,600. You take the gross income (£24,000), and subtract 10% (£2,400) for wear and tear as well as a month's rent (£2,000) for potential void periods.

This gives you a net rental income of around 3.9% (£19,600 / £500,000). This number is very useful as you can now compare it to the interest you might get on a bank account, the return you might make on another asset such as a share, or the return on a different property.

Capital growth

The rental yield is not the whole story. When we consider how good an investment a given property might be, we should obviously also consider potential capital growth – the chance that the price of the property will increase.

Let's take the above example again. Imagine that, as has been the case for some years in many property markets, the price of the property increases. Let us assume it does so by 5%, going from £500,000 to £525,000 in one year.

So, in this example, the return from the property is 3.9% from rental income and 5% from capital gain. We can say that the total return is 8.9%. Not bad. Except that those of you who have been paying close attention should realize that there are a few more pieces of the puzzle to include in our calculation before we can be confident that we have the right number.

Inflation again

Hopefully many of you will have realized that we must account for inflation. If we do not, then we are suffering from money illusion, as mentioned above. If inflation is also 5%, say, then your capital gain has only kept pace with inflation.

A simple calculation of the real return you make on your property is:

Net rental yield + capital gain – inflation.

In this example, this gives us: 3.9% + 5% – 5% = 3.9%.

Without wanting to complicate things too much, also bear in mind that inflation will affect the value of your rental income throughout the year. With inflation at 5%, the £2,000 you receive in rent at the end of the year is worth about £100 less than it was at the beginning of the year. Your *real* return is, therefore, a little bit lower still.

Tax

You may already have thought of yet another thing to be aware of: tax. Wherever you are in the world, there will more than likely be various property taxes to contend with. Depending on where you live, these might include tax on any income you make from the property, tax on any capital gains you make when you sell it, and also annual taxes based on the value of the property. To ensure you have an accurate idea of the income you might be able to generate from a property and, by extension, what it might be worth, you will need to take these into account too.

And, finally, the cost of money

Perhaps most important of all, most people will need to borrow money from a bank in order to buy a property. This is what a mortgage is – a loan that is used to buy property. When you take out a mortgage, you have to pay interest on that money.

To keep the maths easy again. In the £500,000 example we have been using, quite often, you might have bought this property with a £50,000 deposit in cash and then borrowed £450,000 from the bank using a mortgage. If we assume the interest rate on that mortgage is 5%, then you will be paying the bank £22,500 in interest payments each year (0.05 × £450,000), which is £1,875 a month.

So your real return, after accounting for inflation and the cost of money, is actually going to be negative in this example. You're making £24,000 in rent, subtracting £4,400 for void periods and wear and tear, and paying £22,500 of interest on your mortgage. This doesn't include any of the taxes you will have to pay either.

Of course, very often the *real* return on property has been positive. If rental income or capital growth, or both, are a good deal higher than in the example given above, then you have a good chance of making a solid real return on property, but this doesn't always happen.

Property and borrowing money: a key point

One very important feature of the property market is that it is the one asset that most private individuals can borrow a lot of money to buy. This means that if property values increase in real terms you can make a great deal of money, as lots of people have in many countries in recent years.

This is because of something called 'leverage' or 'gearing', which basically just means using debt to buy something.

Using the same example as above, where you have invested £50,000 and borrowed £450,000 to buy a property: imagine that the property increases in value to £550,000. This means that you will have doubled your £50,000. If you were to sell the property (for £550,000) and pay the bank back their £450,000 loan, you would have £100,000 left over. In this example you have made 100%, because you have turned your £50,000 deposit into £100,000. Crucially, you have made this fantastic return even though the property itself has only increased in value by 10% (from £500,000 to £550,000). This is obviously great, and a big part of the reason that lots of people love to invest in property. The bank is essentially helping you to make a bigger return by lending you enough money to buy something you could otherwise not afford.

Set against this, however, it is important to consider what happens if the price of the property does the opposite. If this property *falls* in value, say to £450,000, you will have effectively lost *all* of the £50,000 you invested. Even though the property itself has only fallen in value by 10% (from £500,000 to £450,000), you have lost 100% of the money you put into it.

It is very important to understand this aspect of property investment. Being able to borrow money from the bank is a double-edged sword. It will magnify your gains, but it will also magnify your losses.

This is why it is *really* important to understand all the things we have just covered in some detail before you buy a property. Perhaps the most important thing of all to understand is the difference between nominal growth in property prices and real growth – growth after you've accounted for inflation.

If a property has doubled in price over a few years, but the value of money has halved over the same time period, you will have enjoyed nominal growth of 100% but real growth in your actual wealth of 0%. All too few people understand this reality when it comes to property investment.

It is true that property will often perform better than cash held on deposit in a bank account, because the rental yield and capital gain is more than the real interest rate (after inflation) you will earn on money sitting in a bank.

It's worth taking a step back, however, to reiterate a point I made earlier just in passing. Just because things have been a certain way for many years does not mean they will always be that way. If interest rates and inflation are higher in the future than they have been in the past, property returns could be much lower, and possibly even negative in real terms. This has been the case in many times and places throughout history and is something you need to be careful about, particularly if you're going to borrow lots of money from the bank!

Demographics

Another thing to think about when it comes to property prices is something called 'demographics',[2] and most particularly how many old people are in a given property market. For example, if there are lots of young people just starting out on their careers in a given time or place, then there will likely be higher demand for cheaper properties for 'first time buyers'. If there are lots of people in their forties or fifties, likely earning the most they will ever earn, there will probably be more demand for more expensive properties. Crucially, if there are lots of very old people, there could end up being quite a lot of property for sale.

To explain why this is, and without wanting to sound too morbid, remember that when somebody dies, their home will often have to go up for sale. This is because there can be taxes to pay when people die, and those taxes can often be too much for their children to pay without being forced to sell the family home. Or maybe one of the children isn't wealthy enough to buy out their siblings, so the property has to be sold so that all of them can get their inheritance money.

[2] This is the scientific study of population statistics.

This is particularly the case in the UK. Today there are more than two and a half times as many people in Britain over the age of 90 compared to 30 years ago.[3] As more of these people die in the years ahead, many of their properties will have to go on the market so that their children can afford to pay the inheritance taxes that will come due. If there aren't enough wealthy, younger people to buy all of these properties as they come onto the market, the overall price of property could fall.

Ratio of house prices to salaries

The other key metric we looked at earlier, which can help you work out roughly how affordable property is at any given time, is the ratio of house prices to salaries. Usually this calculation uses some kind of average house price compared to some kind of average salary. This could be for a particular city, region or even for an entire country.

For example, if average annual income in the US is around $80,000 and the average property costs about $400,000, which is roughly correct at the time of writing, then you can see that the ratio here is five times ($400,000 / $80,000 = 5).

A national average tells you *something* but is probably not as useful as looking at a more specific area, such as the city you might want to live in. This can sometimes tell a very different story than the national average. For example, the average income in Los Angeles at the moment is around $100,000 a year, but the average property in Los Angeles is more like $1,000,000. This makes the ratio in Los Angeles around ten times, and shows just how expensive it is to live there.

In London, things can be even more extreme. Average annual income in London at the moment is around £45,000, depending on the data you use. This compares to average property prices of as much as £700,000, implying that properties in London are as much as 15 times incomes at the moment!

---

[3] https://www.ons.gov.uk/peoplepopulationandcommunity/birthsdeathsandmarriages/ageing/bulletins/estimatesoftheveryoldincludingcentenarians/2002to2020

Mean reversion

Another very important idea in finance generally is something called 'mean reversion'. As you may know, the 'mean' is just a type of average. 'Mean reversion' is the idea that many financial assets will tend to go back towards their long-run average (or 'mean') price over the medium to long term.

When we think about the ratio of house prices to salaries, therefore, it is useful to know what the long-run averages have been. For much of the last two centuries, in many parts of the US, UK, Australia, and elsewhere, property prices tended to be around three to four times salaries. This is a lot lower, as we've seen, than what properties cost in those places today.

There are lots of reasons that this is the case. The main two of which have been:

1 Interest rates in recent years have been very low, and much lower than they were historically. Interest rates and house prices are 'inversely related'. That is to say: the lower interest rates are, the higher house prices will be. This is because if it becomes cheaper to borrow the money you need to buy a property, people have more money and can pay higher prices.
2 It has become quite a lot easier to borrow money in recent decades. Historically, it was quite hard to get a mortgage, certainly a big one. In recent years, for all sorts of reasons which are too complicated to go into in any detail, it has become rather easier for people to borrow money.

These are the main reasons that house prices are now a much higher multiple of salaries than they were in the past.

None of us has a crystal ball and we can't *know* whether property prices are likely to 'mean revert' back to being cheaper than they are today, but it is at least useful to understand that they *are* currently very expensive compared to historical trends.

If interest rates are higher in future than they have been in the past and there is less money available, then there is at least a chance that prices may not continue to go up, and may even fall. This has happened in the past. Demographics may also have a role to play with aging populations in so many parts of the world and fewer young people able to afford such high property prices.

As traders like to say: 'The cure for high prices is high prices.' What they mean is that eventually if people can't afford to pay high prices, they will fall.

Whatever happens, if you have read and taken on board the information we have covered in the last few pages, you will now have a much better understanding of property than a lot of people. All too few people understand this stuff before making huge financial commitments that can last many years. The more you know, the more likely you are to avoid getting yourself into financial difficulty.

Renting vs buying

It's worth quickly addressing a couple of well-known statements head on. Is it really true that renting is just 'throwing money away' or 'paying someone else's mortgage'? The answer is 'not always'. We have already seen how it is entirely possible that buying a property will lose you money in real terms (after inflation), especially since property prices won't necessarily continue to go up the way they have in the past.

There are plenty of reasons why renting may be a sensible thing to do. Sometimes it can even be considerably better in financial terms than buying.

Let's go back to our example from earlier in this chapter: a £500,000 property being rented for £24,000 a year.

Imagine that there is a correction in house prices and they fall 10%. This means that the property is now worth £450,000. This is roughly equivalent to two years of rent. This means that you could have been better off renting than buying that property for at least two years, even before accounting for inflation. Remember, too, that if you'd put down a £50,000 deposit to buy the property, you would have lost all of that money.

There tend to be lots of other costs involved when you buy a property too. First, there is that large deposit, which can take a long time to save up. If you use that deposit to buy property it means you can't use it for any other kind of investment. Economists call this an 'opportunity cost'. By putting a big chunk of your money into the property, you have lost the opportunity to put it into another kind of investment, which might have made you a better return.

In addition, the very basic rent calculation I just gave also doesn't take account of the significant transaction costs – lawyers, surveyors, realtors and so on – you have to pay when you buy a property, or the taxes which are charged in many places when the transaction is completed. These can add up to a lot of money. When you buy a property, you will also very likely have significant set-up costs such as buying furniture and large appliances, and you will also need to take care of ongoing maintenance and insurance costs, which can be steep. When you rent, a lot of these costs are borne by your landlord, not by you.

Renting can also give you far more flexibility in your life, particularly if you're not yet 100% sure where you want to live. In an increasingly mobile world, it may not be ideal if you end up spending all the money required to buy somewhere and then realize you want to move to a new city or even country not long afterwards. Of course, you can always rent out a property you own when you do this, but this can be pretty stressful and involve a lot of work and added cost. You may not even cover your mortgage in a weak market.

Perhaps the most important thing overall is not to feel pressure about 'getting on the property ladder'. At the very least, you should do a proper analysis of the 'right' answer for you, based on your own personal circumstances, wishes and desires.

Buying a property can be a great thing to do. But so can renting, particularly when you are young. The key thing is to never let the whole subject be a source of stress or worry. There can be huge 'FOMO' (Fear Of Missing Out) when young people see their friends buying properties and they're not yet able to. It is well worth guarding against this feeling, and making sure that you make decisions based on what is best for *you* in the long term. When it comes to making decisions about property, you should absolutely think in terms of decades rather than just the next few months or years.

Big picture: how much should you spend on putting a roof over your head?

Perhaps the simplest way to think about property is to use a basic rule of thumb that you should only ever spend around one third of what you earn each month on it, if at all possible, whether you are renting or buying. This idea has been around for a very long time. Remember, this was part of the whole idea of 33/33/33 we looked at earlier – and George S. Clason came up with in the 1920s.

Interestingly, in France, there is something called the 'rule of thirds' (*règle des tiers*) when people look to get a mortgage and buy a property. In the French market, banks tend to ensure that people's monthly mortgage payments should not exceed one-third of their net monthly income (after tax).

This is quite different to how many English-speaking markets have behaved in recent decades, where quite a lot of people have chosen to pay a significantly higher percentage of their monthly income than that. In the UK, for example, it is not unusual for a married couple to spend some way more than a third of their *combined* monthly income on mortgage payments.

This feature of the French property market has made it a great deal less volatile than many markets in English-speaking countries. According to the French National Association of Real Estate Agents (FNAIM), French property prices fell around 10% in the global financial crisis as compared to as much as 30% or even 50% in some parts of the UK and the US.

It is important to note that suffering a 30% or 50% fall in the value of your property at some point in your life can be hugely stressful and very damaging to your ability to become wealthy over time.

Hopefully this section of the book has given you some of the tools you need to think quite deeply about the decisions you make around property and increase the chance that you avoid suffering this sort of outcome. Armed with these various valuation methods, you have a far better chance of making the right decision about when to buy a home and at what price.

Of course, there is an emotional angle to buying a home that should be taken into account as well. Property is the only asset where this factor should have an impact on our decision-making process. That said, if you want to maximize your chances of building wealth throughout your lifetime, you should not be afraid to be patient and rent if the metrics and considerations we have looked at in this section of the book suggest that the asset you are looking at is historically expensive.

If you find yourself looking for property and the only ones you like are priced at a very high multiple of your income, or even possibly a high multiple of the income of you and your significant other combined, then you should almost certainly consider renting for the time being.

If spending no more than one-third of what you earn on putting a roof over your head means you have to spend a few years living in a slightly less 'flash' place, or a less fashionable neighbourhood, so what?

Similarly, if this means that you need to rent, even for quite a few years, this isn't something you should be ashamed of or something that should be a source of stress or anxiety. Life is a marathon, not a sprint and, when it comes to money, the tortoise tends to beat the hare, as we have seen.

As a general comment, and as we shall see in the next section of the book, you will be best served by ensuring that you are able to invest in assets other than property as you go through life. This will be very hard if you spend too much on where you live. If the only investment you have in your life is property, or if you're spending a huge amount of your disposable income on rent, then you are likely missing out on lots of other opportunities to grow your money, and your financial situation is likely to be fundamentally imbalanced.

Spending the right amount on where you live increases the chance that you will be able to become wealthy in the medium to long term.

All of that having been said, if you are living at home with your parents and you are particularly keen to get your own place, then you might consider spending a little bit more on rent to begin with. If you think there is a good chance your earnings will increase in the reasonably near future, and you're really keen to enjoy the independence of your own place, then you can perhaps relax the idea of spending no more than a third for a few years, perhaps in your early twenties for example.

If you do things properly, in the long term you will be able to have a lovely home, spare cash and the peace of mind that you can afford it.

7
First things first – paying down debt and saving some cash

In the last chapter we looked at how important property is when thinking about your finances. In the next few pages we are going to look at each of the other main kinds of investment. Before we do that, however, there are a couple of key first steps on the road. Before you invest, you need to do two really important things:

1 Make sure you don't have any expensive debt.
2 Save up a certain amount of cash for a 'rainy day' pot.

Dealing with credit and debt

Given that this book is aimed at a slightly younger audience, you may never have used any debt. That said, one of the reasons so many young people struggle financially nowadays is because they take on too much debt at a young age, often before they really understand how it works and how dangerous it can be for their financial future. This can create huge problems. Getting this wrong can cast a shadow over your life for many years, and make it much harder to become wealthy.

It is not an exaggeration to say that there is something of an epidemic of young people getting into trouble with debt, particularly in the developed world. Credit cards have become very easy to get hold of and there has been a huge growth in the culture of 'buy now, pay later'. This is very good for banks and credit card companies, but can be very bad for you if you get into this sort of trouble at a relatively young age.

In Chapter 3, when we covered compounding, we looked at how frighteningly quickly debt can grow. We compared compounding investment returns, which will make you richer, against compounding debt, which will make you poorer very quickly. As we saw, if you borrow for long periods of time at high interest rates, you can end up in a lot of debt.

So, it is important for us to have a quick look at the subject of debt and things like credit cards and store loans before we go on to look in more detail at investing overall.

If at all possible, you really should do your best to avoid using credit cards, unless you absolutely have to. Human beings managed without them for centuries after all, and tended to do their best to live within their means and spend less money than they earned.

Nowadays this approach is pretty unusual, but that doesn't mean that it isn't something you should try to do. Your life is likely to be much better and far less stressful if you succeed. All too many people are buying things they don't really need and can't really afford. This can make life a great deal harder over time, and will certainly make it much more difficult to become wealthy.

As the American writer Will Rogers famously joked:

> Too many people spend money they haven't earned to buy things they don't want to impress people they don't like.

Make no mistake, this is a bad idea. It isn't difficult to argue that people all over the developed world spend a lot of money on things they don't really need or even want. Studies have shown that the average American throws away as much as 100 pounds (more than 45 kilos) of clothes every year. Many clothing items are worn fewer than ten times.[1] This causes billions of pounds of waste, most of which isn't reused or recycled. In the UK, the average British household has 20 unwanted electrical items and Britons throw out 22 million pieces of furniture each year.

The household storage industry has grown enormously on both sides of the Atlantic for years. Millions of people in the US and Europe are paying to store huge quantities of things that they don't use and that they didn't really want in the first place.

Think about how much useless stuff you buy – and what might have happened if you invested all that money instead. These are choices that can and will have a huge impact on whether you become wealthy or not.

One way to get around this problem is to use the '72 hour' or 'one week' rule every time you think you want to buy something. If you've got your eye on a new pair of shoes, a TV, a gaming console, or whatever it might be, force yourself to wait somewhere between

---

1 https://www.wastemanaged.co.uk/our-news/retail/fashion-waste-facts-and-statistics/

three days and a week before you click 'buy'. Ask yourself whether you really, really need it. Often, waiting a few days will give you time to think more carefully about whether buying that thing is the right choice. This can help you develop better habits around money and minimize the amount of useless clutter you build up over time, too.

Morgan Housel is an American author who has written one of the best books on finance in recent years, *The Psychology of Money*, which has sold millions of copies. He explains that *real* wealth is something you can't see. People can't see the financial assets that you have accumulated that will make you rich and give you real freedom and peace of mind. This compares to the things you can see, such as designer clothes, big TVs, luxury cars and so on, which actually make you poor even if they make you *look* rich.

Housel makes the point that, more often than not, the people who appear to be wealthy, because they have all sorts of stuff, are not actually wealthy at all, and are often heading towards disaster. As we've seen, many celebrities are in this boat. It is important to keep this in mind over the years, if you want to be wealthy. Wealth comes from the money you don't spend.

If you do decide to use a credit card, the ideal approach is only using it for convenience and perhaps to get things like points or airmiles which you can use to improve your life. You should do your very best to pay off any balances every month to avoid paying interest and accumulating debt.

At the very least, you should always make sure you make the minimum payment on time each month to avoid late fees and penalties. Whenever possible, you should do your best to pay more than the minimum to reduce your balance as far as possible so you can save on interest.

Also, if you are going to use a credit card, make sure you shop around for the lowest possible interest rates. Lower interest rates will reduce your overall cost of borrowing and make it easier to manage your repayments.

If you've built up credit card or other expensive debt in the past, you might consider taking advantage of a new credit card with a 0%

APR[2] to reduce your interest whilst you attempt to clear that debt. You could also secure a consolidation loan to reduce your interest payments and simplify things with one monthly payment.

Overall, you really should do your very best to avoid overborrowing. Only borrow what you need and what you can afford to repay. Overborrowing can lead to a debt spiral where repayments become unmanageable and can be a huge source of stress.

As another general comment, it is really important to make sure that you understand the terms and conditions of any debt you take on, including interest rates, fees, and repayment schedules. This can help you avoid unexpected charges and limit how fast you get into debt.

If you have expensive debt, you're not ready to invest

Perhaps the most important thing to understand here, is that if you have credit card or other expensive debt, you are not ready to *invest*. You have to pay down any expensive debt before you can start growing your money. This is because the interest rate your credit card or loan provider will charge you on your debt will almost certainly be higher than the return you can make on investing, unless you are very lucky, very clever, or both of those things.

Investing in anything whilst you still have expensive debt is not a good idea. Putting money into any kind of investment whilst you still have costly debt outstanding is like filling a bath with the plug hole open. The water disappears down the drain faster than the tap can fill the bath!

As you get older, there are certain types of cheaper debt where this may not apply. The most common of these are student debt and mortgage debt. It can be sensible to make investments at the same time as having student or mortgage debt, but it is important to understand this stuff in some detail.

---

[2] 'APR' stands for 'Annual Percentage Rate', which is the yearly cost of borrowing money on a credit card, expressed as a percentage. For example, if you borrow $1,000 at a 25% APR, that will cost you $250 just in interest payments.

If the interest rate on your debt is lower than the return you can make on your investments, then there is a chance that the bath can fill faster than it empties. The most obvious potential example of this is mortgage debt. Many working adults will want to save and invest at the same time as they are paying off a mortgage.

But the broad points still stands; before you are ready to invest and grow your wealth in your life, you need to make sure you don't have any expensive debt outstanding. If you don't do this, there is a high chance you won't make any forward progress financially and investing will be a waste of time or even really quite damaging for your finances.

Hopefully this shows how important it is to be careful about how you use debt, particularly when you're young. As boring as this might sound, particularly if you're excited about getting started with investment, you should allocate any spare cash that you've managed to find to paying down any expensive debt until that is done.

Build up a 'rainy day' pot of cash

The next thing to consider is that you should not begin to invest any money into the sorts of financial assets we will be looking at in the next few chapters of this book until you have first paid off any expensive debt *and* saved up some cash.

Most experts in personal finance suggest that when you start saving, you should keep 100% of those savings in cash until you have built up a 'rainy day' pot. It is best to always keep a certain amount of cash in your life as soon as you can and maintain that reserve for the rest of your life.

Far too few people do this. It is estimated that 22% of American households have no savings at all and 56% would be unable to cover an unexpected bill of $1,000.[3] In the UK, nearly 9 million British adults have no personal savings at all, and 46% have less than £1,000.[4]

[3] https://finmasters.com/savings-statistics/

[4] https://www.finance-monthly.com/2024/01/the-average-savings-based-on-your-age/

This causes people a great deal of stress. Research shows that nearly 25 million British adults began 2024 worrying about money.[5] In the US, nearly 2 in 3 Americans say they are more worried about running out of money than death![6]

This is why a very important first step on your financial journey is to save up a decent 'rainy day' pot. This might take a while but it is really important to do, nevertheless. When you start to earn any money, the first thing to do is build up that cash pot. Ideally, you will want to keep saving until you have enough to fund your life for a few months even if you aren't earning any money.

Only once you have done this are you then ready to begin to invest money into the sort of financial assets we will discuss next.

---

[5] https://moneyadvicetrust.org/latest-news/4-7-million-starting-new-year-feeling-unable-to-cope-due-to-money-worries/

[6] https://www.allianzlife.com/about/newsroom/2024-Press-Releases/Nearly-2-in-3-Americans-Worry-More-about-Running-Out-of-Money-than-Death

8
Investment vehicles / asset classes

'Personal finance isn't that hard.'

Ramit Sethi, best-selling author and founder of the personal finance blog *iwillteachyoutoberich.com*

So far in this book we have looked at how important money and investment are, big picture. If you want to maximize the chance that you become wealthy at least!

The next thing to get to grips with is the different kinds of investment that exist. These are sometimes called 'asset classes' or 'investment vehicles', each of which you can use to store and (hopefully) build wealth.

No doubt you will have heard of some of these already. They include things like cash, shares and property (often called 'real estate'), for example. But there are a few others that are perhaps less well known, such as bonds, currencies (otherwise known as 'foreign exchange'), and commodities.

You will also almost certainly have heard of a new kind of asset class that has received a great deal of attention in recent years, particularly from younger investors: namely crypto.

It's worth listing all of them here in one place before we go on to look at each in detail. The main types of individual investment vehicles, or asset classes, you will want to learn about are:

1 Cash
2 Property (or real estate)
3 Bonds
4 Shares (otherwise known as 'stocks' or 'equities')
5 Commodities
6 Funds
7 Currencies (or foreign exchange)
8 Crypto.

If you want to become wealthy, it is important to have a basic understanding of each of these things.

The importance of funds

For the majority of private investors, funds are arguably the most relevant of these investment vehicles. This is quite simply because a fund allows you to own a large basket of any of the other products on the list, or even a mix of them from several categories.

As an investor in a single fund, you can end up owning hundreds or even actually thousands of shares. In certain types of funds, you might even end up owning a mixture of shares, bonds, property and commodities. This is very important for a number of reasons, which we will look at in more detail in a moment.

As ever, do not worry that there is too much to learn. The list might look daunting, with no fewer than eight categories of investment products to understand. Don't worry. It is true that you could read dozens of books on each and every one of the categories listed above; it's also true, however, that you will be able to arrange your finances successfully and grow your wealth without having an in-depth grasp of any of them. You really don't need to know in any great detail what a share or bond is, or how commodities trade, in order to improve your financial position. That said, it is key to have a *basic* understanding of what each of them is, if only so that you can better understand the suggestions that follow later in the book.

Asset allocation

Another thing that is very important, and which I should highlight at the start of this chapter, is having a rough idea of what proportion of your wealth you want to have in each of these categories. Dividing your money across the different investment vehicles is what is known as 'asset allocation'. Asset allocation is actually one of the most important things to be aware of when investing, but it is something that far too few people understand or even think about. It is also something that changes as you get older, as we shall see.

When you are young, you want to be looking to grow your money. As you age, however, you will want to ensure that you are investing more and more safely to preserve the money you have already made and earn a decent income from it. At the simplest level, this means that the older you are, the more of your wealth you should hold in bonds and cash, and the younger you are, the more in shares (equities). To give yourself the best chance of becoming truly wealthy, you need to ensure that you are aware of, and are exposed to the right sort of *mix* of investments.

A general comment on all of these asset classes

Each of the investment vehicles listed above has certain individual characteristics, but arguably the two most important things for you to be aware of when you're looking at any of them are:

1. How safe your money is when you invest
2. What sort of percentage return you might expect to make.

Put another way, as you learn about, and eventually look to make different types of investments in the real world, you will want to think about the return *of* your money and the return *on* it!

Again, it is worth stressing that you don't need to have a massively in-depth understanding of each of these things. Becoming an expert in any one of them is a huge job, and there are many thousands of finance professionals all over the world who have spent a great deal of time learning to do just that.

All you need is to understand a little about each of them: what they are, how safe they are and what sort of return they might give you. So, with this in mind, let us look very quickly at each in turn.

Cash

When you think about cash as a kind of *investment*, what you generally mean is any money that you have on deposit with a financial organization of some kind. The most obvious example of this is a bank, but there are other similar organizations that are called different names in various parts of the world. Credit unions, savings and loans associations (in the US) and building societies (in the UK) all fall under this umbrella.

'Cash' is also quite obviously the word we use to describe what you have in your pocket, wallet or purse, but we are thinking about cash as an *investment* here.

There are two main reasons that you might keep cash with a bank or other similar financial company. First, for safekeeping: it is generally a better idea to have your cash on deposit somewhere safe, rather than keep lots of it lying around wherever you live, where there is always the risk that it gets stolen or lost.

The second reason is the more important one, however, and this is the fact that if you keep your cash with a bank, you should be paid at least some *interest* on that cash.

When you keep money on deposit at a bank or building society, they will pay you a certain amount each year as a reward for keeping your cash with them. This is what 'interest' is. To keep the maths easy, let's say that they are willing to pay you 5% interest on your savings. This would mean that if you kept $1,000 with them, at the end of the year you would find that this had magically grown to $1,050. A year later, you would have $1,102.50. As we saw earlier in the book when we covered compound interest, over many years, earning interest can help you make really solid progress with your money.

The reason the bank is willing to pay you interest when you keep money with them is because they can then lend out your money to people who want to *borrow* money, and they can charge them a slightly higher interest rate than what they pay you. This is one of the main ways that banks make money. The difference between the interest they pay their savers and the interest they charge their borrowers is generally not an enormous amount, but when you're doing that with many billions of dollars, pounds, euros or whatever, it all adds up, which is why banks can be quite profitable businesses.

It's worth taking a moment here to say a few words in defence of banks and bankers. In recent years, 'bankers' in particular have not been the most popular people in our society, as you're probably aware. I think it is important to stress that the services they provide – lending money to people who need to borrow it, and paying interest to people who want to save – are hugely important for our economies and for human progress too.

Without banks and banking, we wouldn't be able to earn interest on our money, and there wouldn't be money available for providing mortgages and loans to millions of people and businesses so that they can buy homes and build things like office buildings, factories, ships, concert venues and so much else besides. What they do is very important for all of us. As we saw earlier in the book, if there were no banking system and no money or capital markets, human beings would still be very poor and we wouldn't have been able to enjoy essentially any of the wonderful progress we have seen in the last few centuries.

Banking is also a very complicated business, as you might imagine. Every day, most banks in the world are dealing with money coming in and going out from many millions of customers, whether private individuals, businesses or governments. They have to manage this whole process and make sure they always have enough money available to keep providing their services. They have to deal with frequent movements in interest rates and dozens of different currencies, run extremely expensive IT systems, employ lots of staff, and deal with very complicated laws and regulations. They also have to plan for lots of people and businesses who don't pay them back when they borrow money, which makes this all the more difficult still.

When people express their anger about 'bankers', they're choosing to focus on a truly tiny minority of people in the industry. More often than not, such criticisms, born out of ignorance and jealousy, are made by people who have very little understanding of banks and banking. There are hundreds of different kinds of jobs in a bank: traders, salespeople, IT professionals, 'corporate finance' and 'M&A' specialists, and lots else besides. Plenty of these jobs aren't particularly well-paid either. Most people who 'hate' bankers have no nuanced or detailed understanding of what any of these people do. The vast majority of them are perfectly honest and hard-working individuals. They are doing important jobs for the efficient functioning of our economies, for all of our benefit. If you hear friends being rude about 'bankers', it might be worth asking them to be more specific about precisely what they mean by the word. More often than not, they will have no clear idea!

So, when it comes to 'cash' as an investment vehicle, because you (sadly) don't get paid interest on what you carry around with you or hide under your mattress, it is sensible to keep as much cash as you can with a financial organization of some kind.

One of the great things about cash in a bank account is that it is basically secure. Unless there is a huge financial crisis, massive natural disaster, war or revolution, you should always have access to any money you have in a bank account.

Also, most of the time, the amount of money you have in that account will not suddenly be much less one day than it was the day before because the market has crashed. 'Cash doesn't crash', as the saying goes.

Another important point to understand, however, is that because cash is seen as being so safe, the percentage return you can make on it as an investment (i.e. the interest rate) tends to be quite low.

As always, don't forget inflation!

That is pretty much all we need to know about cash as an investible asset: it's all about the interest rate. But before we move on to the next investment vehicle, there is one other key factor we need to be aware of when thinking about cash: inflation.

When considering how safe your money is on deposit at a bank, you must understand the difference between the interest rate your bank is paying you[1] and the real return[2] you are earning on that money, after taking inflation into account. You can calculate your real interest rate by taking the interest rate your bank is paying you and subtracting the rate of inflation.

So, for example, if your bank is paying you an interest rate of 5%, but inflation in your country is currently 3% – your *real* interest rate and return on that money is actually 2%.[3] The precise calculation is actually a bit more complicated than that, but this simpler version will give you a decent approximation.

When we looked at inflation earlier in the book, we saw that real inflation as experienced by most people is probably even higher than the numbers provided by the government. The broad point here is

[1] This is called the 'nominal' interest rate.

[2] This is the 'real' interest rate – after inflation.

[3] 5% *nominal* interest rate minus 3% inflation = 2% *real* interest rate.

that you're unlikely to make much of a *real* return on cash as an investment, because of the true rate of inflation.

You may have heard the saying 'cash is king'. As you will hopefully understand from what we've just explained, this isn't a particularly helpful way of thinking about the world, if you want to become wealthy at least.

It is important to have *some* cash to cover short-term expenses, and you need to have a 'rainy day' pot as we've already seen. It is also best to keep whatever cash you have at a bank or other financial organization as we've just explained. If you want to make higher returns and maximize the chance that you can grow your money, however, you need to make sure you know about and are making use of some of the other kinds of investment! With that, let's turn to those other asset classes.

Property

We looked at property in some detail a few pages back. When you think about the return *of* your money, it is probably pretty obvious that property tends to be one of the better asset classes.

A house, apartment, or other kind of property will always have some value, because there is always demand for places to live and work, and it is almost certainly never going to be worth nothing at all (as can happen with a share), unless you're unlucky enough to live through a revolution or a war! That said, as with so many investments, it is important to understand how to value property to give yourself a fighting chance of buying it at a good level over time.

We looked at rental yield, capital gain and property prices as a multiple of salary in Chapter 6, so there is no point in going over those again, but it is worth remembering that these metrics enable you to compare property as an investment to all the other kinds of investment we are looking at in this chapter.

There are a couple of additional points that are worth making here. First of all, as we have seen, many people in places like the UK and the US have a very high percentage of their net worth, or in many cases all of it, tied up in their property.

One of the most important things you need to bear in mind if you wish to grow your wealth in the safest way possible is asset allocation – using the right mix of different investments over time. If you already have a huge percentage of your net worth tied up in property, you should probably focus on investing in *other* asset classes before you consider *another* property investment. This will obviously depend on the returns you think you can achieve after inflation when you compare the various different options, but it is certainly something to bear in mind.

There are two other categories of property investment to think about over and above where you live: commercial property and foreign or overseas property (and overseas commercial property, for that matter). It is often the case that there will be interesting opportunities in either or both of these categories, and these may be worth considering even if you already have a large percentage of your wealth invested in your own home. One of the best ways of getting exposure to overseas and commercial property is through owning a fund. We shall look at funds in more detail shortly.

As we saw earlier, another key feature of the property market is that it is possible to borrow money to invest in it. This is more or less a unique feature of the property market. At the very least, it's a great deal easier to borrow money to buy property than it is to invest in other asset classes like shares or commodities.

Mortgages enable individuals to 'control' an asset with a value significantly more than the deposit they have saved. In a strong market this is obviously great news for the investor, as we've already covered, but don't forget the point I made a few pages back about how using debt can be a double-edged sword. In a bull market, when prices are going up, you're able to use the bank's money to grow your wealth.

In a bear market, however, when prices are going down, if you have borrowed to purchase a property that then loses value, you can lose all the money you put in. In a really bad market, it can actually be even worse than that.

Consider the example we used earlier in the book – the £500,000 property you bought with a £50,000 deposit. If that property falls in value to £450,000, you will have lost 100% of what you originally invested (your deposit). Imagine, however, that things get really bad and the same property falls in value to £400,000. In this scenario, not only have you lost all of the money you originally invested, but you now owe the bank an additional £50,000 on top of what you'll get if you sold the property! (Your mortgage is £450,000 but you'll only get £400,000 if you sell.)

Negative equity

This is something called 'negative equity' – which just means that your property is worth less than the money you have borrowed to buy it. Negative equity is one of the reasons that people can go very wrong with property investment, so it is really important to at least be aware of it before you decide to invest in property.

As a general rule, the fact that you can borrow money in order to buy a property means there are opportunities for the smart investor to make great money doing so. It is crucial, however, to make sensible assumptions about what might happen to the value of what you buy and to the cost of the money you borrow.

A big part of why the 2007–9 financial crisis happened was because many millions of people assumed property would always appreciate in value, and also only really thought about their monthly payment today, rather than considering what might happen to that monthly payment, and to the value of their property, in the years ahead.

I hope that the points I made earlier in this book will help you reduce the risk that you make the same mistake.

Bonds

The next big asset class that you need to have a basic idea about is the bond market. You're probably already familiar with the idea of a loan: someone – say a bank – will lend you a certain amount of money. After a given amount of time you will pay them the money back, plus an agreed amount of interest to compensate them for being without their money for that time. This is why it is helpful to understand interest rates as the 'cost' or 'price' of money. Fewer people are familiar with bonds, but they are simply:

a loan divided up into many pieces so that it can be made by lots of people.

Imagine a big oil company plans to build a massive new refinery and needs $1 billion to do that. They might go to a big bank and ask for a $1 billion loan. If the bank were particularly relaxed about the strength of that oil company, they might simply lend them the money and ask for an appropriate interest rate as compensation.

More likely, however, they would feel that $1 billion was too large an amount of money for a single company to owe them and that the deal was too risky for them to do by themselves. This being the case, they might do one of two things:

The first approach would be to ask other banks if they would be interested in lending some of the money. Let's say that they find nine other banks that are happy to lend $100 million each, or four other banks that are happy to lend $200 million each. The $1 billion overall deal would then be known as a 'syndicated loan' because a group (or 'syndicate') of banks has clubbed together to reduce their exposure to the oil company, but ensure that the deal still gets done. In this scenario, not only would the original bank receive interest on its loan, but it would also charge a fee for organizing the syndicate. This is one of the things an investment bank does.

The second option would be to print many pieces of paper, each one of which would represent a small fraction of the value of the $1 billion loan, and to offer those pieces of paper for sale to anyone who was interested in providing that small fraction of the loan and receiving interest as compensation.

This is essentially exactly the same process as the syndicated loan, except that the pieces of paper are called 'bonds' and their existence means that the loan can be 'syndicated' (shared) between hundreds, or even thousands, of investors all over the world – rather than just a small group of banks.

For this example, let's say the bank prints a million bonds, each of which is worth $1,000 (for a total of $1 billion), and the oil company commits to paying 5% interest on those bonds. When the bank offers these bonds for sale, potential investors can buy as many or as few of them as they like. For each one that they buy, the oil company will owe them $1,000 plus 5% interest. The interest paid by a bond is referred to as its 'coupon'. This is because in the past, when a bond

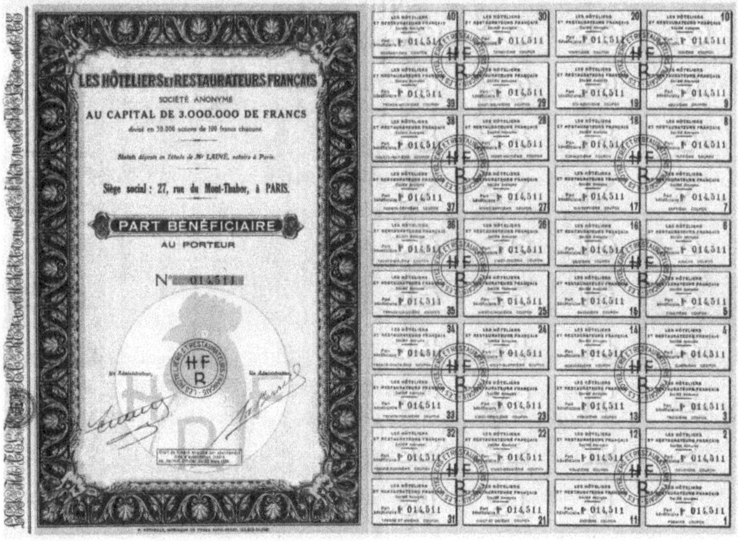

FIGURE 2 An old bond with a coupon © Shutterstock

was literally a piece of paper, it had a detachable coupon for every interest payment the owner was entitled to receive.

If you bought a bond that was due to be paid back in three years and that paid 5% interest by paying the holder 2.5% twice a year, there would have been six coupons. When bonds were originally invented, the bondholder would literally have taken those coupons to a bank every six months and exchanged them for the cheque or cash equivalent to 2.5% of the value of the bond. Today these payments tend to be automated (unless they are payments from what are called 'bearer bonds', which fans of 1980s movies and Bruce Willis may recall were what the criminals were after in the film *Die Hard*).

An important feature of bonds is how long the buyer is lending the seller money for. A bond may entitle its owner to 5% a year and their original money back in three years, five years, or even longer. Some government bonds last as long as 50 years and up.

The secondary market for bonds

Another important thing to understand about bonds is that there is something called a 'secondary market' for them. Say you purchased $10,000 worth of oil company bonds in the example above, but a month later you read that the oil company is in financial trouble. Or, perhaps you just need your money back suddenly. You might decide you would rather have your money back than hold on to the bonds and collect your interest payments. Luckily for you, it is likely that somewhere out there in the world there is someone who still thinks the oil company is a good bet and would like to own your bonds and collect the interest. As a result, you will be able to sell your bonds to that person via an intermediary such as an investment bank.

One important thing to bear in mind at this point is that it is pretty unusual for a private or 'retail' investor (like you) to buy bonds directly. Many bonds, whether issued by a company or a government, trade in amounts that tend to be too big for the average private investor. Because of this, you would usually look to get exposure to bonds by owning a bond fund, which we will look at in more detail shortly.

Government bonds

The next important thing to say about bonds and the bond market is that they are a government's main source of money other than taxation. This is really important to understand, particularly if you care about politics and how governments spend money.

Governments all over the world have essentially only two ways of raising money to pay for the vast array of things they want to fund. The first is taxation. Most of us understand taxes reasonably well. We all pay tax in a wide variety of obvious and not so obvious ways, and the companies we work for and from whom we buy products and services do, too.

However, since taxes were created thousands of years ago, very few governments have been able to survive on what they have taken in tax. Historically, the primary reason for this failure of governments to survive on tax revenue alone was the cost of waging war. War costs a huge amount of money. Ships must be built; soldiers must be paid and supplied. These costs are what led to the invention of the bond market a few hundred years ago.

For the last several centuries, in times of emergency or war, governments have been forced to spend significantly more than they earned in taxation. They have made up the difference by selling bonds to their population and, more recently, to foreign investors including other governments.

There is basically no other way for a government to raise money apart from taxation and selling bonds to investors. A rare exception to this would be when a government sells assets such as land, gold reserves or property – like embassy buildings or military bases, for example. These sales are obviously not a *recurring* income stream and tend, as a result, only to be used in emergencies. Governments can be pretty bad at this. In the UK, for example, former Prime Minister Gordon Brown sold a large proportion of the UK's gold reserves close to a record low.

Sadly, even though most countries have enjoyed unprecedented peace since the end of the Second World War, nearly all Western governments still make a regular habit of spending far more than they are able to raise from taxation.

Nearly all governments in the world have made up the shortfall by selling bonds – that is to say, by borrowing money. (Remember that a bond is just a loan divided into lots of little pieces.)

You might be surprised to learn that for a long time this policy was entirely sustainable. Banks offering mortgages, loans and credit cards are obviously comfortable offering debt products to wealthy individuals who enjoy high annual earnings. There is a very good chance that those individuals will pay back their debt. In the same way, investors all over the world have tended to be fairly comfortable lending money to the governments of countries with high and usually rising annual 'earnings' by buying their bonds. Translated into the language of the bond market: investors have been happy to buy the government bonds of countries with strong and growing economies.

'Risk-free'

Financial theory assumed, until very recently, that lending money to the government of a developed country like the US, the UK or

France was 'risk-free'. If you were to buy $10,000 of bonds from the US government for your pension, for example, you assumed there was no chance at all that you would not get your money back plus the interest promised. After all, the US government was assumed to be so big and rich that no one even considered for a moment the idea that they wouldn't be getting their money back. Even if some incredible catastrophe were to occur, the US government would still be able to print as many dollars as it liked.

In fact, printing money is precisely what many governments are doing today and have been doing for some years. Many of them can no longer afford to pay bond investors the interest and 'principal' on their bonds without inventing new money to do so. The trouble with inventing lots of new money out of thin air is that it creates inflation. As a reminder, if you double the supply of pounds, dollars, yen or euros but the supply of 'stuff' remains fixed, you will not create any more wealth but instead will simply double the price of everything, all other things being equal. This is why any policy of inventing money out of thin air is counterproductive and doesn't make anyone wealthier in real terms in the medium to long run.

Whilst investors all over the world continued to believe the bonds of wealthy nations were essentially risk-free, they were prepared to earn pretty low returns on those bonds. Given a choice of places to invest your money, you may be willing to accept a lower return on 'risk-free' money, which you feel you are guaranteed to get back, than you are on a riskier investment where you worry you may not!

Part of the whole crisis of the last few years is that, increasingly, investors all over the world no longer see the bonds of many developed countries as 'risk-free'. This is a very important change, as it has an impact on interest rates and inflation. Let us look quickly at why this is.

Government bond prices and interest rates

There is a key relationship between bond prices and interest rates. Imagine that the US government is selling a one-year bond worth $100 and offering to pay $5 of interest. This means that, if you buy the bond, you are entitled to $100 of capital (the principal) and $5 of interest at the end of the year.

If you pay $100 for this bond, your return on that investment will be 5%. This should hopefully be easy to understand. You pay $100 and after a year you get $105 back. A simple percentage return calculation shows us that this is 5%.

However, in the 'secondary market' that we talked about earlier, bond prices constantly move up and down depending on what investors all over the world feel about the country or company that issued (sold) the bonds. As such, you can end up paying more or less than $100 for 100 dollars' 'worth' of bonds.

In the example above, if you were to pay $101 for the bond, your return would end up being just below 4%. This is because you are now losing 1% of your capital (you paid more than $100 for the bond but only get $100 of capital back at the end of the year), and your percentage return on the $5 of interest is a tiny bit lower than before (5/101 instead of 5/100).

If you were to pay $99 for it, your return would be a tiny bit over 6%. This time you are making a bit more than 1% on your capital (you paid $99 but receive $100 back at the end of the year), and your $5 of interest represents a slightly higher fraction of $99 than it does of $100.

Lower bond prices mean higher interest rates and vice versa. They are two sides of the same coin.

This is very important to understand. Governments that need to raise money to pay for all the things their tax revenue can't cover must sell bonds to investors at home and abroad to make up the difference. If those investors are less confident about the financial strength of that government, they will be prepared to pay less for that country's bonds. This means that the price of the bonds falls, and lower bond prices mean higher interest rates. More accurately, lower bond prices *are* higher interest rates.

The general point here is that governments have rather less power to set interest rates than many people realize. This is because the massive global bond market, which is made up of thousands of big investors from all over the world with trillions of dollars, pounds, euros, yen, etc. at their disposal is more powerful than pretty much every single country in the world when it comes to setting interest rates.

Even the US government has far less power to set interest rates than you might think.

If the global bond market doesn't want to buy a country's bonds, that country will have to cut the price of those bonds until someone will. This drives interest rates up (because lower bond prices = higher interest rates).

What countries that control their own currencies, such as the UK and the US, can do in this situation is invent new money out of thin air to buy their own bonds, as crazy as this sounds. This is something called 'quantitative easing', or QE for short, which you may have heard of in recent years.

QE can keep bond prices artificially high, and interest rates artificially low as a result. The problem is, however, that this tends to create inflation. When governments do this, they can keep interest rates low and raise money to spend on things but the value of the money they raise will reduce, because of inflation. This is precisely what has been happening for the last several decades.

Why do governments want to keep interest rates low?

There are a number of reasons why governments in most places in the world want to keep interest rates lower than what the natural bond 'market' level should probably be.

Falling bond prices are something of a vicious spiral: as interest rates rise, the government needs to pay more to borrow money, making investors even less willing to invest in that country's bonds as they worry about the financial strength of the government.

High interest rates also put the brake on an economy for the following reasons:

- People are less inclined to take out a mortgage or take on other forms of debt. This depresses the housing market and the retail sector.
- Those who have a variable rate mortgage see their monthly payments go up and have less to spend as a result, which means the rest of the economy suffers. If interest rates increase too much, people may even end up being forced

to sell their homes – something we may see a great deal of in the next few decades, sadly.

- Companies are less likely to hire people or invest in a new factory or piece of equipment. If borrowing money is more expensive, then they will make fewer investments overall.

Any government that has mismanaged its financial affairs will find itself having to drop the prices of its bonds in order to sell enough of them to get the money it needs. This results in the extremely unpopular and economically damaging reality of higher interest rates, as the alternative is not being able to raise money on the bond markets at all.

Given that neither of these options is a vote winner, plenty of governments throughout history have gone with the other option I have just mentioned: inventing money out of thin air to buy their own bonds.

It is very important to understand that inventing money out of thin air has been attempted dozens of times throughout history and has been described in various ways ('debasing coins', 'printing money', QE). It has almost always resulted in economic disaster for the country or society involved, in the long run at least. This has included: ancient Rome, Weimar Germany in the 1920s, Argentina and many other Latin American countries in the 1980s and 2000s, and most recently Zimbabwe – home to the $100 trillion note, as recently as 2009.

FIGURE 3 A $100 trillion Zimbabwean note © Alamy

For most of history, places like the US and UK didn't play this game. Their economies were strong enough that they could pay back their debts with real money, and could keep bond market investors happy buying their bonds at low interest rates. They didn't need to invent any money out of thin air. Sadly, this is no longer the case. Both the US and the UK have had to resort to inventing money to buy their own bonds in order to keep interest rates artificially low.

As we have already seen, inventing money causes inflation. If you have basically the same amount of stuff in an economy and the quantity of paper money doubles, the price of that stuff will also double (generally after a certain time lag).

This is because inventing money does not cause any more stuff to be created – more oil to be found or wheat to be grown, for example – and therefore the supply of stuff remains the same (in the short run at least), but the amount of money everyone has to pay for that stuff increases.

What this means for you, is that if the government doubles the amount of money in existence in order to buy its own bonds and avoid dealing with the consequences of its previous actions, you will need your employer to double your salary just to stand still financially! How likely do you think that is?

We have already seen the following quote from John Maynard Keynes, but it bears repeating again to really make the point now we have a better understanding of what he meant:

> By a continuing process of inflation, governments can confiscate, secretly and unobserved, an important part of the wealth of their citizens.

This is exactly what is happening. If you think that the idea of a government doubling the money supply is far-fetched, think again. In 2000, something called the M2 money supply in the US was about $4.7 trillion. By 2023, it had reached nearly $21 trillion.[4] In the UK, the number was below £1 trillion in 2000 and is now just over £3 trillion.

As we can see, the UK government has tripled its money supply and the US government has *quadrupled* its money supply in the last

---

[4] https://www.statista.com/statistics/187729/total-us-money-stock-for-m2-since-1990/

two decades. They've done roughly the same with total levels of government debt. At the same time they've done this, as we saw earlier in the book, because of the way they calculate 'inflation', very few people understand what *real* inflation is and how bad all of this is for their *real* wealth as a result.

Many politicians really don't understand this stuff

Even more worrying than all this endless money printing and misleading inflation numbers, however, is the fact that many of our lawmakers simply do not understand these issues.

We've seen plenty of evidence to this effect. In the original version of this book, I highlighted a story about a US congressman, sitting on a key finance committee in Washington, listening to arguments from academics and finance professionals. After an hour or so he put his hand up and asked: 'Sorry, but what is this "QE" you keep talking about?'

The fact that an elected politician, sitting in the US government and partly responsible for making US financial policy (a policy that affects you!), asked this question is absolutely shocking, and goes some way to helping us understand why we are in the state we are in. We saw a similar performance from the US Senate more recently when Mark Zuckerberg, the CEO of Meta / Facebook, was asked questions that showed that many key policymakers had absolutely no understanding of how the internet works!

It's not just the US; the same can be said of plenty of politicians elsewhere, including in the UK. As crazy as it sounds, many of the people in charge on both sides of the Atlantic have no idea what they are doing, financially speaking. They just don't understand the economics.

Once you have finished reading this book you will likely understand more about finance than many politicians and political journalists in the US and the UK.

While a US congressman or British MP working on economic policy mustn't be forgiven for being unfamiliar with the term QE, I think it is entirely fair that you might not have come across it before reading this book. Understanding this concept is another string to your bow in terms of being able to improve your financial situation. To paraphrase an earlier quote: those who understand QE are destined to make money from it, and those who don't are destined to suffer.

Bond default

One final aspect of bonds that is important to understand is that unless the company or country issuing the bonds goes bankrupt they are legally obliged to pay the bondholder their money back, plus the agreed-upon interest. If a company or government cannot pay this money back due to bankruptcy, this is known as 'default'. Default in the government bond market has been relatively rare. It is more common with corporate bonds – bonds issued by companies – for obvious reasons.

Given the relative rarity of government default, bonds have traditionally been viewed as the safest financial investment you can make – similar to keeping your money in a deposit account. You are almost certain to get back your original money plus the agreed-upon interest.

The downside is that the return you make is small, particularly after accounting for real inflation. If inflation is running at 5% or more, for example, then you will be losing *real* wealth if you own bonds that provide you with a return of less than 5%. For bigger returns, you will have to look elsewhere. One of the first places to go looking for higher returns is with stocks and shares, otherwise known as 'equities'.

Shares / equities / stocks

Most people are aware of the existence of stocks and shares but few really understand what they are, including many who invest in them. This is clearly bad news, and it's another reason why people think investment is riskier than it need be.

One of the first things worth highlighting is that the words 'share', 'stock' and 'equity' all mean basically the same thing, so don't be put off by all the different terms (typical of the finance industry to describe the same thing at least three different ways!).

The next key point is that if you want to become wealthy, it is really important to understand and make use of the stock market throughout your life. Sadly, far too few people do this, primarily because most people have no detailed understanding of what it actually is. Stocks are arguably the most important asset class of all, at least for building real wealth over time.

Similarly, all too many people who *do* get involved with the stock market do so before they really understand anywhere near enough about what it is or how it works. This is one of the reasons all too many people lose money when they invest in shares. It also explains why, when surveyed, a large percentage of the population think the stock market is a fundamentally risky thing and is best avoided. This is a tragedy and it really needn't be this way. All you need is a little knowledge.

Perhaps the best way for us to grasp the idea of 'shares' at a fundamental level is to have a quick look at how and why they came about historically. Along with the debt market and bonds, shares were an extremely important development in human history.

It is not an exaggeration to say that without their invention, the Industrial Revolution and the enormous technological and social developments billions of us have enjoyed in the last few centuries, which have made life so much better for all of us, would have been impossible.

This is because the invention of the *stock market* enabled large groups of people to *pool resources* and *spread risk* to achieve things that one person or a small group of people could not have achieved on their own. It is important to understand that the 'stock market' is actually just a *technology* to concentrate capital and spread risk.

The idea of the 'joint-stock company' came about in the Netherlands and Britain in the early 17th century. The Dutch and the British were great maritime powers that wanted to get out and about and explore the world. The problem was that sending fleets of ships to places like the Americas and Asia cost vast amounts of money and had very uncertain outcomes as you might imagine.

Sea voyages invariably took years and in that time there was a high risk that ships would be lost along the way. It soon became clear that even the aristocrats and royal families of Europe couldn't afford to fund these sorts of voyages of discovery by themselves. Building, equipping and crewing ships was just far too expensive.

The solution was the creation of something called a 'company'. 'Shares' in that company could be sold to anyone who was interested in investing. Essentially this meant that an investor who contributed, say, 1% of the costs associated with a voyage would be given a piece of paper that recorded their entitlement to a share of 1% of any profits made.

The difference between a share and a bond was that a shareholder had no *guarantee* of a return. Someone buying a bond was essentially guaranteed to get his or her money back (plus the agreed-upon interest) unless the bond issuer defaulted, as we saw in the section above. Someone buying a share was only entitled to their percentage of any *profits* the company made.

If the ships all came back to Amsterdam or London with valuable cargo, shareholders could have made their fortune. If, on the other hand, the fleet was decimated by storms or piracy, shareholders might find that they had lost all the money they had invested.

By sharing such enormous costs over a large number of people, however, this outcome wouldn't be a complete disaster for each individual involved (as long as they invested only what they could afford to lose).

This whole idea was nothing less than an enabling technology and truly revolutionary. Without it, very little economic progress could have been made in the time since. To really bring this point home, it is worth looking at when the stock market was invented, and then at what humanity has achieved since then!

Look around your home, your street, your local grocery or drug store, and think about how few of the things you are looking at would exist without the stock market.

As much as 80-90% of the things around you at this very moment didn't and couldn't exist two centuries ago, because we didn't have the fundamental technology of the stock market. Without it, we couldn't bring enough capital together to do amazing, risky things. It is worth stressing just how important the invention of shares has been for our development and progress as a species.

Without the invention of the stock market and the funding it provided, there would be very few large commercial buildings, no aviation, no automotive industry or modern roads, no cutting-edge medicine, no films or TV, no Italian olive oil or Argentinian wine or Scottish steak in your local grocery store, and very few if any of the small daily luxuries that we take for granted, like toothpaste, toilet roll, running water, inexpensive clothing, and so on.

Without the fundamental technology of the stock market, 80% or more of us would very likely still be subsistence farming, and life would be a hell of a lot poorer, harder and shorter.

The stock market has quite clearly been one of the greatest inventions in human history. It has lifted billions of people out of poverty, saved them from malnutrition and increased their lifespans. It has increased our comfort and given us more leisure time and travel. It has been largely responsible for making the world a fundamentally more peaceful, interesting and healthy place.

Stock markets facilitate the sharing of risk amongst thousands of individuals and organizations, and allow the concentration of a sufficient amount of capital to be focused on one extremely complex task in order to get that task done. No single individual could afford to invest enough or accumulate all the skills needed to provide any of the things listed above, or to create the microchip, fibre optics, the smartphone or artificial intelligence.

Without wanting to get too political, it is more than a little annoying when multi-millionaire celebrities bang on about the supposed evils of stock market capitalism. All too often it seems more or less clear that such folk feel this way despite having no understanding of what they're talking about. As a classic example of this, in his 2014 book *Revolution*, the British comedian Russell Brand described stock markets as 'bollocks',[5] despite admitting on the very same page that he knows nothing about them!

Such people quite clearly don't understand in any powerful or detailed way just how much the stock market has delivered for our species in the time since it was invented. They've never had any first-hand experience of what equities are all about and don't understand how they work, by their own admission!

[5] An excellent British word.

They've never thought deeply about what has had to happen in the forests and paper mills of Scandinavia or Canada, and in the shipping and trucking industries of Europe and the US, and about what has been spent on building a massive network of convenient retail outlets just to get toilet paper into their homes, for example, let alone the tens of thousands of other amazing products we have today that 99% of humans who ever lived didn't have, and that so many of us take entirely for granted.

Communist systems simply cannot provide anything like the same, based on the very clear evidence of history. This is why people in places like communist Russia and present-day North Korea had or have very few of the things we take for granted in modern Western democracies, and have been grindingly poor and very often hungry or even starving, too. It is also why so many millions of the citizens in such places have died throughout history. It is estimated that somewhere between 6 and 10 million people died in the Soviet Union under Stalin as a result of his agricultural policies alone, for example. The number who died in China was even higher. A failure to understand this reality is genuinely dangerous for everyone's future standard of living, whether you are rich or poor, and for human progress as a whole.

Another important and related point to make about stock markets is that they have been one of the key factors that have made the world more peaceful and less violent in the last many decades than at any other time in human history.

Despite what is happening in Ukraine, Israel, Gaza and Yemen at the time of writing, your risk of having to fight in a war or of dying from violence of some kind is massively lower today than it was for most of the rest of human history, and this is true for the huge majority of the world's population.

The invention of capital markets is a big part of why this is the case. They have connected nation-states together, with the result that the costs of war, in the main, massively outweigh the benefits. The development of the telecommunications and travel industries has also meant that many of us now have friends from countries that were once 'enemies'.

This is why the US will almost certainly never again go to war with Japan, nor Germany with France, for example. Nowadays these nations are just far too economically, politically and socially entwined.

Stock market capitalism is certainly not perfect. No system is. One unattractive feature of the system is that it can result in significant wealth inequality. As we have seen, this has a great deal to do with the mathematics of compounding over long periods of time. Capitalism has also been largely responsible for many of the environmental problems that feature so prominently in our idea of the world nowadays.

That said, it is probably fair to say that too few people understand this stuff and realize in any sufficiently emotive way just how much capital markets have given us as a species and how far we have come as a result.

Because of this, it is also probably fair to say that many people massively underestimate just how much capitalism is evolving and has been a force for good already. There are literally tens of thousands of companies working on solutions to environmental degradation and climate change, for example. All too few people are aware of this. There is a good chance many of these companies can deliver some fantastic results, and sooner than many of us fear, because such technologies are developing exponentially. We already looked at some of these exciting developments in Chapter 4.

Rather than rail against stock markets and capitalism, a far better course of action is to take a little time to understand them and then, crucially, to get involved. Happily, when you buy a share in a company you quite literally become a part-owner of that company. This means that you are then entitled to your proportional share in the company's profits. If you think about it, this is a very exciting and powerful thing. By owning a share in a business, you can benefit from the work of everyone involved.

Stock market investment is also not just the preserve of the wealthy – or certainly should not be; it is available to anyone who is willing to find out about it and get involved. It is this involvement that will give them a much better chance of becoming wealthy themselves.

I would argue, in other words, that the 'causality' runs the opposite way to what many people think. Too many people incorrectly think 'the stock market is only for rich people', when what they should be thinking is: 'If I learn about and use the stock market, I have a decent chance of being a rich person' – or comfortably off at the very least.

As we have seen, over time small numbers can become big numbers because of the power of compounding. As a result of this 'eighth wonder of the world', arguably the richest 1% of people in the world today are generally quite simply the most economically and financially literate 1% of people, and the ones with the best financial habits; they are simply the ones who have learned about and 'do' investment over long periods of time, and even more so when done over many generations.

This is truer today than at any other time in history, primarily because it has never been easier to become an owner of businesses.

The British newspaper *The Sunday Times* publishes a 'Rich List' of the wealthiest 1,000 people in the UK each year. In 1989, when it was first published, a significant percentage of people on the list had inherited their wealth. In the 2018 edition, however, the newspaper noted that 94% of the people on the list were 'self-made'.

Of course, we can all argue about what 'self-made' means. It is certainly fair to say that many wealthy people have had significant educational and other advantages. But many haven't. Taylor Swift's father was a financial adviser at the large investment bank Merrill Lynch when she was growing up. He was likely better placed to be supportive with nice guitars and studio time – and no doubt with navigating things like legal agreements – than the parents of other aspiring singers from less affluent backgrounds. But for every Taylor Swift, there are plenty of examples of extraordinary people who have come from rural villages in India, or from extremely poor backgrounds in all sorts of other places, but who have still managed to become wealthy by building businesses and investing over decades.

I'm not suggesting that everyone can become a multimillionaire, or that it is easy, but if you can't beat them, why not join them by becoming an investor in companies just as they are, even if on a smaller scale?

Single stocks vs entire markets

Getting involved with stock market investment is one of the highest probability ways to become wealthy over time. That said, all too many people lose money when they do it. There are many reasons for this, but the main one is quite simply because too many people don't learn enough about the market before they get involved.

One of the rookie mistakes so many people make is to invest in *single shares*, that is *individual companies*, without understanding how to do that well. The evidence shows that a lot of investors only own a small number of single shares.

Nowadays this might be something like one or two of Tesla, Meta (Facebook), Amazon or Alphabet (Google). Or, even worse than that, a small number of really high-risk stocks that a friend might have told you supposedly have great prospects. All too often, this is a very dangerous approach to stock market investment. This is because buying single shares is a very complicated and expert thing to do.

To explain: it is important to understand that before you go anywhere near buying an individual share, you will be best served by producing a detailed checklist of all the reasons you want to buy that share.

To be able to do this, you will need to understand a huge amount about stock market investment, accounting and company economics. You might find the next few paragraphs a bit boring and technical, but they are really important so you can understand in a really powerful way just how much is involved in single stock investing, so please bear with me.

Before buying a single share, you will want to have a really solid understanding of everything that follows in the list below:

- You will need to understand something called 'valuation metrics'. These metrics have scary names like P/E and EV/EBITDA ratios, Return On Capital Employed, Earnings Yield, Dividend Yield, PEG ratios and a fair bit else besides.
- You will want to be up to speed on something called 'balance sheet metrics'. This accounts for how much debt a company is using and the value of its various assets. This will include something called 'gearing ratios' and the current value of 'tangible' and 'intangible' assets on the company's balance sheet. You will also want to have a view on whether those assets have been valued appropriately.
- You will want to know the revenue, profit and earnings numbers for the company, and what growth in those numbers has been like in the past and is likely to be in the future.

- You will need to be aware of the things the company is expected to do in the next few years – the 'news flow' they're likely to have.
- You will need to think about the various 'macro' factors that might affect the company. This includes geopolitics, changes in government, regulatory stuff, tax changes, currency risk and so on.
- You will want to be mindful of what professional investors might call other 'exogenous' factors: what are competing companies doing? Is there a new technology or trend that could threaten the company's business? Netflix killed off the video rental business Blockbuster, for example, and digital photography and smartphones did the same to the camera and film company Kodak Eastman. Both of these were very big companies once upon a time, and then they went to zero.
- You will also want to think about something called 'M&A' (Mergers and Acquisitions). This has to do with whether the company might get bought or whether it might buy other companies.
- You will need to know about the management of the company. How good are they and how committed? Do they own lots of shares themselves or not? How much do they pay themselves and how is their pay calculated?
- You will want to be aware of the company's position vis-à-vis stock market *indices*. Is the company part of an index? Might it fall out of that index? If it is not in an index, might it be included in one any time soon? This will create buyers or sellers from index investors. (I will explain more about what an index is shortly.)
- You will want to have a think about what the current shareholder register looks like. How smart are the other shareholders? How long have they been involved? What sort of investors are they? Where are they in the world?
- If you're really good, you should also know a fair bit about a number of various technical indicators for the company's share. These include even more complicated and

scary-sounding things like RSI, MACD, Bollinger Bands and average volumes traded over a certain period of time.
- Plus, you will probably want to have had a look at what forecasts are doing across most of the above.

No matter what, you should also have an exit plan. The laundry list of stuff we've just gone through can give you a reasonable measure of confidence to *buy* something. How are you going to decide when to *sell* it, though?

Most amateur investors never even think about this when they buy a share, but deciding when to sell is arguably even more important than when to buy, if you want to make money!

So, let's pause for breath after that fairly exhausting list of complicated, technical stuff! How many people do you think know about everything we have just gone through? The evidence is that very few people do this work before buying and selling shares, and that is why stock market investment can be so dangerous.

Make no bones about it, if you don't understand everything we've just looked at in real detail, you *really* shouldn't be making investments in individual shares. At the very least, you should realize that, if you do, what you are doing is very risky indeed and probably better described as gambling and not investing.

Even incredibly smart and well-resourced professional investors who *do* understand all of these things can lose money when they invest in shares.

The good news is that this need not be a problem. It shouldn't prevent you from investing in the stock market, for the simple reason that you can buy the entire market.

For most investors, investing in an entire stock market is a far better option than learning the huge amount that you need to learn before you can invest in single shares with any level of confidence and sufficient skill.

Buying an entire market has a number of advantages over investing in single stocks:

- It does not require you to spend a huge amount of time learning about all the complex stuff I have just described. (Phew!)

- It ensures that you are 'diversified' across a large number of companies and industries.
- It takes relatively little time and effort.
- It is also very cheap to do – and can be tax efficient in many countries.

The evidence shows that the majority of investors underperform the stock market – they make lower percentage returns than the market does overall. So why not just buy the market? This will increase the chance that you do better than most investors, by definition!

As the veteran American investor John Bogle put it:

> Don't look for the needle in the haystack. Just buy the haystack.[6]

To buy entire markets, all you need to do is understand what an index is and how you get exposure to that index by using something called a tracker or Exchange Traded Fund (ETF). We will look at this in more detail in the last section of the book when we look more at the specifics of how to invest.

That's all we need to know about shares for the moment. Let's move on to our next major asset class.

Commodities

You probably have some sense of what a commodity is, but it is still worth clarifying precisely what the term means. One source describes a 'commodity' as:

> A good for which there is demand but which is supplied without qualitative differentiation across a market.[7]

[6] John C. Bogle, *The Little Book of Common Sense Investing: The Only Way to Guarantee Your Fair Share of Stock Market Returns*, 10th Anniversary Edition, updated and revised. John Wiley & Sons, 2017.

[7] CORE, *The Economy: Economics for a Changing World*, Unit 8 – Supply and Demand: Price-taking and Competitive Markets, 2017, https://books.core-econ.org/the-economy/v1/book/text/08.html. Last accessed 1 August 2025.

Although this might sound a little complicated, all it means is that something like oil is basically the same whether it is supplied by the US, Nigeria, Russia or Venezuela.

Compare this to something like a car, where the value and price you pay will vary a great deal based on things like brand, top speed, engine size and finish quality.

Commodities have been used as a store of value throughout human history, and many commodities have also been used as money. The word 'salary' comes from the fact that Roman soldiers were originally paid in salt (*sal*), as we saw right at the beginning of the book.

The points we are going to look at here are basically relevant to all commodities, but it is worth noting that it is useful to think of the precious or 'monetary' metals (gold and silver) as a separate category from all other commodities. This is because they continue to be accepted as money to a certain extent. This has not been true of any other commodities for several hundred years. We will look at this important difference in more detail, as understanding it will be one of the things that helps to grow your wealth in the years ahead.

Not that many people think about commodities when they invest. The traditional approach to investing tends to focus in particular on cash, property, bonds and shares. Relatively few people or financial advisers include commodities in their mix of investments. This is potentially quite a big miss, because they can be another excellent string to your bow when it comes to growing your money.

Why you should think about commodities

There are a number of reasons why you should include commodities in your thinking today. Here are three of the main ones:

1 There is huge growth in the *demand* for commodities

In December 2022 there was a great deal in the news about the fact that the global population had reached 8 billion. Much the same thing happened only 11 years earlier, in October 2011, when the 7 billionth human was born. It only took just over a decade to add a billion more human beings! The world's population is currently growing by around 70 million people per year – nearly 200,000 per day – and this growth will likely continue for the next few decades.

Just as important as this incredible growth in population, is the fact that an increasing number of these people are getting wealthier. In China 30 years ago, hardly anyone had a car; there were no high-speed trains and hardly any skyscrapers. Today, the Chinese buy millions more cars per year than the Americans, have more miles of high-speed train track than anywhere else in the world, and have thousands of skyscrapers, and many more planned or in construction. This has obviously had a huge impact on the market for commodities, particularly those used in the automotive, rail and construction sectors.

Until very recently, most people in the developing world also survived on very simple diets and could afford very little meat. Now millions more Chinese, Brazilians, Indians and so on consume chicken, fish, pork and beef. This ongoing trend has very serious implications for global agriculture and water supplies. As millions of new consumers grow up and become richer all over the world, the overall demand for commodities of all kinds will likely grow as a result.

2 THE WORLD HAS SOME SERIOUS CHALLENGES WITH THE *SUPPLY* OF COMMODITIES

At the same time that there is this big increase in the demand for commodities, the world is beginning to encounter serious supply constraints for many of them. For example, the volume of rock a mining company has to dig through to find one ounce of gold today is a multiple of what it was only a few years ago; miners now create several tonnes of waste just to produce one wedding ring. Most of the biggest gold mines in the world, in places like South Africa, for example, are seeing supply dry up. This is hardly surprising when you consider they have already been dug to a depth of 3–4 kilometres!

Much the same is happening for nearly every metal we use: copper, zinc, platinum, silver and so on. We are finding it harder and harder to find new supplies of all these things. The same is true in the oil market, where companies are having to go to extraordinary lengths to find new oil. Many energy experts believe that the 'cheap', relatively easily accessible oil we relied on for generations is now essentially gone. The era of cheap oil is now almost certainly behind us.

We are also inevitably running into supply constraints with 'soft' commodities (things that live and grow) as the world exhausts its supply of arable land, fresh water and fish in a bid to feed so many billion people. This will only get worse as people in the developing world increase their meat consumption, as livestock farming leads to far more water and land use than growing crops.

Basic economics tells us that when demand for something is increasing and supply is decreasing or fixed, then the price of that thing must go up; this should be fairly obvious. If more people want something but there is less of it available, they will have to offer more money than the next person to get hold of it. This goes some way to explaining why so many commodities in the world have seen a significant increase in price in the last few decades. This being the case, we can conclude that the fundamental, structural (inherent) trend in commodities will likely be for their prices to increase over time, even if not in a straight line.

3 The supply of new paper money drives up prices

There is another reason why commodity prices (in terms of paper currency) look set to carry on rising. As we have seen several times already, governments all over the world have produced vast quantities of new money. We have already seen how the supply of money has more than tripled in the US in recent years. If you triple the supply of money but the supply of things is basically fixed, then the price of those things should triple, after some time has elapsed.

This is another reason why the dollar (and pound, yen and euro) price of almost all the 'stuff' in the world has increased rapidly in the last few years. While governments all over the world continue to pursue a policy of printing (or 'inventing') money, commodity prices – priced in those currencies – will tend to increase.

If your income in these paper currencies is basically fixed (which is the case for most people), this is very bad news for your standard of living. If your income this year is the same as last year, but bread, eggs, milk, fuel and so on have increased in price by 20% or even more, it should be clear that you will suffer a reduction in your *real* standard of living. This is precisely what has been happening all over the world for several decades, especially during the COVID-19 crisis.

The great news, however, is that there is something you can do about this: you can own commodities. You might describe this as 'owning inflation' – and this is a key part of 'owning the world'.

Luckily for us, developments in financial products in the last few years have made owning commodities easier and cheaper than ever before. As we've already discussed, it wasn't that long ago that it was actually very hard to buy financial exposure to commodities. This is no longer the case. One of the main reasons we can now buy commodities without too much effort, is thanks to the development of the next – and arguably the most important – category of investment vehicle: funds.

Funds

For the majority of people, funds are the most relevant (and appropriate) investment vehicle. This is because a fund enables you to own a large basket of the other financial products discussed in this chapter.

Buying the right funds over many years can make a huge difference to your life. So what are funds – and, more importantly, what are the 'right' funds to buy?

The first funds in the City of London were invented nearly two centuries ago for a very simple, logical reason. One of the most important ideas in investment is something called 'diversification'. This is simply the investor's version of 'not putting all your eggs in one basket'.

Jack Meyer is an American investor who used to run Harvard University's multibillion-dollar endowment fund. He has said about diversification:

> The most powerful tool an investor has working for him or her is diversification. True diversification allows you to build portfolios with higher returns for the same risk.[8]

Early on in the creation of financial assets, particularly shares, it was clear to anyone with common sense that splitting your money between several investments is inherently less risky than having all your money in one investment. This should make sense to you intuitively. Academic researchers have since confirmed it many times.

It was also the case that many early potential investors were excited about investing in more than just one business area or sector. Why restrict themselves to owning one oil company if they could invest in several oil companies as well as a number of agricultural companies, railway companies, pharmaceutical companies, defence contractors and so on, all at the same time? Why restrict themselves to assets from only one region of the world? By owning a wide variety of companies from a wide variety of countries, not only would they spread their risk, but they would also give themselves exposure to as many exciting parts of the world economy as possible.

It's clear why many people with money to invest were interested in owning a large number of shares in a large number of sectors and countries. The only problem was that there was usually a reasonably large minimum investment required in order to buy any given share. This meant that, in the early days of the stock market, only very rich people were able to own a large number of shares in a large number of sectors. They were the only ones who were able to spread their risk and benefit from owning a greater number of potentially successful companies. This is another reason why the rich found it relatively easy to stay rich.

If you had to invest a minimum of $1,000 in each share, for example, you would obviously have needed $10,000 to invest in ten shares – or $30,000 to own one of each of the 30 stocks in the Dow Jones, an index of 30 of the biggest companies in America. In the early days of

[8] Cited in James B. Stewart, 'A League of Their Own', *SmartMoney* (September 2007), pp. 70–5, at p. 71.

the stock market, this was a huge amount of money for one person to invest. Diversification of any kind was, therefore, only possible for people who were already extremely wealthy.

The genius of funds

Investment funds were invented to solve this problem. The idea was simply to *pool* money from many investors, each of whom were interested in owning a large cross-section of investments. This large pool of money would then be able to invest in lots of different investments. If 10,000 people invested an average of $10,000 each, for example, you would have a fund of $100 million, which could then buy dozens or even hundreds of different shares. In the UK, for example, the Foreign and Colonial Investment Trust was founded in 1868 to 'Help the "investor of moderate means" have "the same advantage as the large capitalist"'.

Everyone who bought shares in that fund would then nominally (theoretically) own a proportion of *all* the shares owned by the fund – even if their theoretical investment in each share was far less than the minimum amount they would ordinarily be permitted to own *directly*.

The other advantage for investors was that the company offering the fund for sale would take care of the administrative pain of owning dozens or hundreds of shares.

As you can imagine, because of the many advantages in terms of diversification and administration that funds gave investors, the idea caught on. Today, there are thousands of investment companies all over the world offering hundreds of thousands of different funds. Companies that offer a range of funds are known as fund managers, asset managers, investment managers or hedge funds. These terms all mean basically the same thing (although hedge funds are slightly different).

You may have heard of companies like BlackRock, Vanguard, Fidelity, Invesco, T. Rowe Price, and so on. There are many thousands more all over the world.

Active and passive funds

As funds became more popular over the years, two main categories of fund developed: *active* and *passive*.

Active funds are funds where an individual (known as a fund manager) tries to use his or her skill to pick the best shares (or other assets such as bonds or commodities) to make the best return possible for investors in that fund.

A fund of this type will usually be limited to investing in a certain type of asset class. For example, it might be a 'European equities fund', in which case the fund manager would be limited to buying shares in European companies. This limitation on what the fund manager can invest in is called a 'mandate'. The mandate on any given fund describes the type of assets in which that fund manager can invest.

Active funds tend to be relatively expensive, as you will have to pay for the 'clever', well-paid fund manager to invest in the 'right' shares, bonds or commodities, depending on what type of fund you purchase.

Some fund managers are excellent and well worth this premium. However, there is a wealth of research that says that, on average over the long run, passive funds outperform active funds (after accounting for costs).

This doesn't mean you should dismiss active funds entirely, particularly as you get older and wealthier. There are certain investments you might want to make that can only really be done with an active fund. But as a general rule, particularly if you are just starting out, and want to keep things simple and minimize your costs, you will very likely be better off using passive funds.

Passive funds copy the performance of an index (see below). These funds are sometimes referred to as 'tracker' or 'index' funds (because they 'track' an index). A good example would be a tracker on the S&P 500.

If you were to buy into such a fund it would aim to replicate as closely as possible the performance of the S&P 500 index of American shares. If you were to invest in such a fund, your money would essentially be divided across the 500 shares in the S&P 500 index. This is a crucial advantage of being in a fund. You yourself would not be able to own all 500 stocks in the index, unless you had a great deal of money and a great deal of time to devote to investment. These days, even the super-rich will tend to use a tracker or index fund to own lots of shares in one place.

Passive funds are a cheaper way to invest than active funds and are a much easier (and cheaper) way to get exposure to a large number of shares than buying those same shares individually.

What is an index?

An index is simply a method of measuring a stock market in some way. (The plural of 'index' is 'indices', by the way.)

The S&P 500 is an index. It's an invention of a company called S&P Global. They add up the price and size of the biggest 500 companies listed on a stock market in the US. The number that results is then known as the 'level' of the S&P 500.

The point of this is to give investors all over the world a rough snapshot of how well the US stock market is doing and how well the American economy is doing, by extension.

The S&P 500 does not represent the entire US economy, but it is a good 'proxy' since the top 500 companies represent a very large percentage of the entire value of the stock market, and the activities of those companies represent a large percentage of the value of the US economy as a whole too.

The S&P 500 index does not tell the whole story about the economy because there are thousands of other, smaller stock-market-listed companies, as well as millions more private companies (that is, companies that are not listed on the stock market), operating in the US.

Every country in the world that has a stock market has several stock market *indices*. These were originally created and managed by the companies in charge of those stock markets (like the London Stock Exchange in the UK or Deutsche Börse in Germany). Indices you may have heard of include: the Dow Jones, NASDAQ and S&P 500 in the US; the Nikkei in Japan; the Hang Seng in Hong Kong; the DAX in Germany; the CAC in France; the ASX in Australia; and so on.

Each national stock exchange chooses to include different numbers of shares in their main index and then cuts their market up in a variety of different ways, providing other additional indices for the investor to look at.

In the US, besides the S&P 500, there is also the Russell 2,000, which includes 2,000 smaller stock-market-listed companies. In the UK, there is the FTSE 100 of the 100 biggest British companies and the FTSE 250, which includes the next 250 companies in terms of size. Together, they make up the FTSE 350.

Indices are very useful to us as investors. If you want to make sure that you own 500 of the most important companies in the US, or the 100 biggest companies in the UK, you need look no further than the S&P 500 or the FTSE 100.

In recent years, independent financial information firms such as Reuters and Bloomberg have created their own indices for a wide variety of assets, as have certain divisions of big investment banks like Morgan Stanley, Barclays and Goldman Sachs.

What this means is that you can now find indices for pretty much any asset or country in the world: bonds, commodities, big companies, small companies, and stock market sectors such as banks, telecoms or pharmaceutical companies.

The reason this is important for our purposes is that as a private investor you are generally able to 'buy' these indices using a related fund. This is what passive index or tracker funds are. The most common of these types of fund, available all over the world, are called 'exchange-traded funds' or ETFs for short. Today, it is possible to invest in pretty much anything that you can think of using an ETF.

To give you an idea of the insane choice out there nowadays, in an article from August 2019, James Mackintosh of the *Wall Street Journal* wrote that:

> There are indexes and ETFs for everything; no one knows exactly how many, but it is certainly in the millions.[9]

9 James Mackinstosh, 'How ETFS swallowed the stock market', *Wall Street Journal*, 30 August 2019, https://www.wsj.com/articles/how-etfs-swallowed-the-stock-market-11567162801. Last accessed 1 August 2025.

This is actually quite amazing. It has literally never been easier in the whole of human history for you to implement any investment idea you might have. Yet another example of my claim that 'human progress' is the most important investment theme of them all.

Set against this, however, is something called 'the paradox of choice'. This is the idea that the more choice you have, the more likely you are to suffer indecision and not actually get the results you want in life – whether you're talking about choosing a song on Spotify, a movie on Netflix or, arguably rather more importantly, what to do about your investments!

For most people, the best way to get around this problem is to keep things as simple as possible. To do this, arguably the easiest approach when you invest is to look to buy into one of the very biggest and most liquid stock markets.

As its name suggests, the S&P 500 index includes 500 of the biggest companies in America, including all the big names you will be more than familiar with, such as Apple, Google, Tesla, Facebook, Microsoft and Amazon, and several hundred others, many of which are also household names like VISA, Mastercard, McDonald's and so on.

At the time of writing, the S&P 500 has delivered an average return of more than 10% a year for more than a century. As you will hopefully remember from when we looked at compounding, if you can make that sort of return on your money over long periods of time, you have a good chance of becoming wealthy.

It's very important to understand that this is an *average* return over a long period of time. That 10% average does not come smoothly every year like an interest rate. Some years the S&P 500 is up as much as 30%. Every few years it crashes and can fall a long way. In big crashes, stock markets all over the world can be cut in half. To seek to achieve that 10% return, or as close to it as possible, you have to be very clear about this, and be investing for the very long run.

We will look at this idea in more detail in the final section of the book when we look at 'how to invest so that crashes don't matter'.

It's also important to understand that past performance is not a reliable indicator of future performance. Just because something was true in history, even for many decades, does not mean it will continue to be in future.

As an example, lots of people investing from the 1850s onwards put their money in the Russian and Argentinian stock markets. This could have been a perfectly sensible thing to do at the time but certainly wasn't for most of the 20th century.

The fact that the S&P 500 has averaged more than 10% for a century is great, but is no guarantee that it will continue to do so indefinitely. Even if it does, it will certainly take backward steps every few years. But, as we've already seen, the reason why it has delivered these sorts of returns over very long periods of time is, quite simply, human progress.

If you believe in human progress, then it is probably a good idea to invest in it. For what it is worth, even if you have doubts about human progress and you're convinced that it's all going to come crashing down as we descend into some kind of World War III, you may as well invest anyway.

Why? Well, first of all because wealthy people have far more power to navigate awful situations like war, but also because if we are unlucky enough to experience nuclear Armageddon in our lifetime, your investment returns up to that point will be irrelevant anyway.

You might as well invest whatever happens because if things continue to develop as positively as they have in the last two centuries, you will be far better off if you do. If our worst fears are realized, it won't matter either way. This is what traders call an 'asymmetric bet'. There is far more upside to investing than not investing, whichever scenario ends up playing out.

So, one option when you think about investing in funds is to invest in the US stock market. It has done very well for the last century as we've seen and buying into it is easy and inexpensive to do. This having been said, there is no guarantee that all the best and biggest companies in the world will come from America in the decades ahead.

The period since the end of World War II has been characterized by something called 'American exceptionalism'. The US stock market has led the charge for some time as a result, and particularly in the last ten years, but, as any smart ten-year-old will tell you, what goes up must eventually come down.

This is a view shared by some very smart people, including Ray Dalio, the founder of Bridgewater, the biggest hedge fund in the world. He made the case that America's best days may be behind it in his 2021 book *The Changing World Order*.

This being the case, might it be a good idea to widen the net a bit and look to invest in more than just the US? There are already a good number of companies from places like Asia and Europe that are in the top few largest companies in the world today. These include: Taiwan Semiconductor Manufacturing Company (TSMC) in Taiwan, Novo Nordisk in Denmark, Tencent in China, LVMH in France, Samsung in Korea and ASML in the Netherlands.

Given how dominant the US has been for the last decade and given the direction of travel in places like China, Europe, India, Latin America, the Middle East and Africa, might it be better to hedge our bets a bit?

The good news is that this is also easy and inexpensive to do. You need look no further than two companies which provide large *global* stock market indices: MSCI and FTSE.

MSCI (Morgan Stanley Capital International) is a company that makes indices. Their MSCI World Index is made up of around 1,500 of the biggest companies from all over the developed world. Their MSCI All-Country World Index includes roughly 3,000 companies, including ones from the developing world as well.

Then there is also the FTSE All-World Index, which includes even more companies from all around the world – developed and developing - with more than 4,000 at the time of writing. You can invest in Exchange Traded Funds for all three of these indices, thus securing exposure to thousands of companies from all over the world, and to human progress, wherever it might come from.

You might argue that there is a good chance that at least some of the success stories of the next ten or 20 years might come from places other than the US. For what it is worth, though, American shares make up a significant chunk of all of these various global indices anyway. This means that, to a certain extent, you can 'have your cake and eat it' here, given that you'll still have exposure to those big US companies should they continue to dominate the world economy.

Funds that own indices for you are a fantastic and powerful innovation, particularly when you consider that you can put very small amounts of money into thousands of companies all at once. They are also a relatively recent innovation. The first big US ones were launched in the 1990s with other big markets following in the early 2000s. They have grown enormously in the time since and it is very easy to invest in them in many parts of the world today.

The long-run returns of these stock market indices can help you become wealthy, but it is still super-important to understand that such things can and do crash every few years. Before you put your hard-earned money to work, it is vital to understand how to deal with this reality and 'how to invest so that crashes don't matter'.

We will cover this in the next section of the book.

Currencies (foreign exchange / forex / FX)

Many of you reading this book will have heard of the foreign exchange (or forex/FX) market. It is quite simply the global market in various currencies from different countries. You will have encountered the 'retail' forex market every time you have gone on vacation and needed to buy pounds, euros, dollars, rupees, or whatever else you needed for your travels. ('Retail' in finance describes a financial service provided to the private individual rather than a company or professional investor.)

As you can imagine, there is a huge need globally for companies, governments and all sorts of other organizations and individuals to change money in order to be able to buy and sell things across borders. As a result, the forex market is by far the biggest financial market in the world.

The Bank of International Settlements estimated in 2022 that more than $7.5 trillion a day is traded in the global currency markets. This number quite possibly underestimates the reality when you consider that there is quite a big black market of illegal currency trading in the world as well!

This vast scale is unsurprising when you think that nearly every single product (oil, cars, TVs) or service (telecommunications, banking, legal services) that crosses a border needs a foreign exchange transaction. In addition, there is an enormous amount of trade in foreign currencies for purely speculative (financial) reasons.

As with any other market, the prices of the assets involved move up and down a fair bit. In the forex market, the assets are the currencies of nearly 200 countries. A country's currency will lose or gain value against other currencies, based on a combination of what is happening in that country and what currency traders expect will happen to that country in the future, just as a share price will move based on what people think about what a company is doing and what they imagine it will do in the future. A share will tend to go up in value if the company is doing well and if people believe that it will continue to do so. A currency will do just the same if people feel the same about the country behind it.

There is always a bull market somewhere

The great thing about the foreign exchange markets is that there is always a bull market somewhere. One currency's strength is, inherently, another currency's weakness, so, no matter what is happening in the world economically, there is always the chance to make money in the forex market if you know what you are doing.

Just as we have seen with other investments, one good thing about the forex market today is that there are ways for the private investor to participate in it that did not exist until quite recently. There are lots of companies that will allow you to trade currencies.

That said, trading foreign exchange is difficult and complicated and it is very easy to lose money. For most people, simply making sure you own assets from all over the world will give you useful exposure to a good number of the world's currencies, without you having to worry about learning how to trade them. You should probably be very careful about getting into forex on your own. I will say more on this subject when we look at the difference between investing and trading in the next section of the book.

Crypto

Another major financial asset class that has emerged in the last few years is crypto. The most famous and best-known crypto asset is bitcoin, which was invented in late 2008. This may seem like quite a long time ago, but not so much when you consider that gold and silver have been financial assets for thousands of years, and bond and stock markets for hundreds of years.

Crypto is arguably the most complicated and controversial of financial asset classes. That said, at the time of writing, the entire crypto industry is valued at more than $3 trillion. It is also something that younger investors are particularly interested in, so it is important to include it in this list of the key investment vehicles.

Crypto is also in the news at the moment because President Trump and his supporters seem to have a much more positive view of it than many politicians have previously.

Explaining crypto in detail would add many thousands of words to this book and, more importantly, waste many hours of your time. There are plenty of other books and resources out there that can give you more detail if you are interested.

We don't need to go down that rabbit hole. The main aim of reading this book is to develop the confidence to get your finances sorted. There is real merit in the idea of 'the fastest route from A to B'. Nevertheless, it is worth having a quick look at some of the main points when it comes to crypto given how interested so many people are in this asset class.

From single- to triple-entry bookkeeping

Perhaps the best 'plain English' description of crypto is that it is a technology that enables triple-entry bookkeeping (or accounting). As we saw right at the beginning of the book, for much of human history, humans were hunter-gatherers and any trade that did occur took place under a barter system. As a result, trade was pretty limited, and humans didn't really make any forward progress in terms of becoming wealthier or more technologically sophisticated for tens – arguably even hundreds – of thousands of years.

Then, a few thousand years ago, some smart folk in what is now modern-day Iraq (the Sumerians, as it happens) invented a transformational technology: single-entry bookkeeping (or single-entry accounting – the terms are basically interchangeable). They figured out how to write down that person x owned something and/or that person y owed person z something.

Archaeologists have found clay tablets dating back to several thousand years BCE that record the fact that a certain individual owned a certain quantity of an agricultural crop. Although this may not seem like much of a breakthrough, it was actually completely transformational for humanity and for our ability to grow economically and technologically.

As the website Hacker Noon (https://hackernoon.com) has put it:

> Once you can keep track of who owns what, trading starts to happen at a much larger scale. That's why the kings and queens of ancient times could build castles and establish professional armies and create great wonders of the world.[10]

The problem with single-entry bookkeeping was that you had to trust the person who was keeping score! Any dishonest 'scribe' in a position of power could very easily alter the record to enrich his friends or family at the expense of the rightful owner of any given property. If history is any guide, this is very often precisely what happened – leading to a great deal of strife and bloodshed.

Fast-forward a few centuries and we find that various human cultures were able to upgrade this single-entry accounting system to a version 2.0. Logically enough, we call this double-entry bookkeeping. Double-entry bookkeeping is the foundation of modern accounting and, without exaggeration, modern civilization. There would be no nation states, no large buildings, bridges, roads, cars, planes, boats, drugs or supermarkets had humans not invented the fundamental technology of double-entry accounting. (Think about this next time you describe accountants as 'boring'. None of the most important or fun things in life would exist without them.)

The way double-entry accounting works is pretty obvious to us 21st-century geniuses, mostly because we have the benefit of

[10] https://hackernoon.com/why-everyone-missed-the-most-important-invention-in-the-last-500-years-c90b0151c169. Last accessed 1 August 2025.

hindsight. In essence, rather than some aristocratic scribe or record keeper being in charge of keeping track of everyone's wealth, there were now two records kept simultaneously – credit and debit, or asset and liability.

Crucially, these records were also now overseen by an independent third party who could mediate between creditor and debtor and ensure that both sides fulfilled their obligations. The independent third party has gone through various guises since the system was invented (think of the moneylender Shylock in Shakespeare's *The Merchant of Venice* as one example), but the two main institutions that underpin any double-entry system are governments / nation states (and, by extension, their militaries) and banks.

Enter triple-entry bookkeeping

The double-entry system has underpinned virtually all human development since roughly the Middle Ages. With the arrival of bitcoin, we may have finally moved into a new era of triple-entry bookkeeping. The main idea here is that the technology behind bitcoin embeds the trusted third party element of the double-entry system (the bank or government) within the technology itself. It does this by encoding the necessary information in a distributed ledger called the 'blockchain'.

That ledger incorporates a record of every transaction that has taken place, and the fact that it is 'distributed' (doesn't sit in one place but reproduces itself in little pieces of code in thousands of places all over the world) theoretically makes the system robust. The security and trust elements to do all of this are enabled by advanced cryptography (writing and solving complex codes) – which is why bitcoin is described as a 'cryptocurrency'.

As you might imagine, the ability to remove banks and governments from financial (and other) transactions is potentially highly transformational, arguably even revolutionary. Given this fact and given the vested interests involved, the arrival of cryptocurrency and blockchain has been met with a very wide range of reactions depending on the audience in question.

Futurologists and 'techno-anarchists' are delighted and see the emerging technology as a catalyst for a bright future where the power of nation states is severely limited and handed back to the people. Governments, central banks and the financial establishment are less sure, especially given how useful such technologies are to criminals and 'rogue states'. As we have noted above, however, this may be in the process of changing, given the arrival of President Trump in the White House for a second term.

Should I own crypto?

Crypto continues to be a controversial asset class. Perhaps the most important thing to decide when you're thinking about it is whether or not to include it alongside the other major asset classes we are covering in this chapter as part of an overall 'own the world' approach to investment.

The broad answer to that question is probably 'yes, but only if you're careful'. It is important to realize that crypto is a very volatile and risky asset class. Allocating money to it is akin to investing in one single risky share or similarly speculative investment.

In practice, this means that you might consider investing 1%, 3% or (at most) 5–10% of any money you have in crypto. You certainly shouldn't ever invest everything in crypto or invest *only* in crypto. That is a very dangerous thing to do, no matter what the price of bitcoin may or may not have done in recent years!

There are two key reasons why you should be quite careful about crypto as an investment.

First, psychology. It is fair to say that lots of people have made fantastic returns in crypto, with bitcoin trading near $100,000 at the time of writing.

Weirdly enough, however, there are far more people who have lost money along the way.[11] Let's explain why this is: making lots of money in a short period of time is very addictive. It also gives people a false sense of how money and investment work in the real world over a long period of time, based on the evidence of history.

All too often, people who have suddenly struck it rich tend to have a very different attitude to risk than those who have not. If you

[11] https://www.bis.org/publ/bisbull69.pdf

have turned hundreds or thousands of dollars into hundreds of thousands or even in some cases millions of dollars very quickly, this will very likely affect your investing personality. It is likely that you will be far more inclined to take more risk!

Rather than celebrate their good fortune by taking their profits and investing them in more conservative and less risky assets, all too many people who have had this experience continue to 'swing for the fences', which increases the chance that the ultimate end result will be that they eventually lose much of what they've gained.

You might be familiar with the famous American author and life coach Tony Robbins. In an excellent 2018 interview with the leading business podcaster Tim Ferriss, he gives an example of a property investor friend of his who was worth no less than $750 million in 2008. That person failed to rebalance his wealth into a mix of more conservative investments and 'put everything on black', ironically enough in the Las Vegas property market. Within a few months in 2008 he ended up losing everything, owing the banks more than $400 million and going bankrupt.

You can see the same kind of psychology at play in the crypto world. People in the crypto world have a tendency to cite point-to-point price moves as performance numbers, as in: 'Look. If you'd bought bitcoin (or ether, or cardano or some "hot" altcoin) on date *y* when it was trading at price £*z* you would have made ten (or 20 or 50 or 100) times your money. You would be a millionaire by now.'

The trouble is that investment returns just don't actually work like this in the real world – that is, in the world of trying to grow your actual wealth over time. The reason for this is in large part due to something called 'volatility' – the extent to which a given financial asset moves up and down in price over time – and how this interacts with human psychology at a fundamental level.

The 'fact' that any asset price has moved from point x to point y over a certain amount of time is only relevant to your ability to make money if you bought that asset at point *x* and, crucially, sold it at point *y*.

If a certain financial asset travels from, say, $1 to $100 over a period of time such as a few years – and does so slowly and surely in a straight line, then you have quite a high chance of making significant positive returns. Perhaps you missed it at $1 but then bought it at, say, $20 or even $50. If it is now at $100, you've still achieved a great result.

But what if during the journey from $1 to $100 that asset has been massively volatile? What if it has often gone up and down by 20% or 30% – sometimes even in a single day? What if it peaked at $200 before coming back down to $100?

When this is the case, there is a very high chance that you will lose money on that asset. You might have bought it at $190 and now be down nearly 50% on your investment. Or, perhaps you bought it at $80 a few months ago, but sold it at $20 when it fell back a long way because you were worried at that point it might be on its way back to $1!

Even though the asset is up rather wonderfully from $1 to $100 (which is of course a 'fact'), back in the real world, there is a fairly high chance that you will actually have lost money along the way. Even worse: you might have to suffer the horrible experience of that asset zooming up to new heights immediately after you sold it in a panic. Volatility makes it all too easy to lock in a large loss and then sit miserably on the sidelines as you watch the thing you sold go up massively.

This has happened to people time and time again throughout history. It happened in the dot-com boom of the late 1990s and the same thing is happening again in an even more turbo-charged way in the crypto space. The more volatile an asset or asset class is, the more likely you will fall victim to all the points we've made already in this book about how important human psychology is.

The fact that an asset has gone from price *x* to price *y* tells one story, but it doesn't tell you anything about the thousands of other stories that have happened to real people in the real world on that journey. For every person who has made a lot of money with a volatile asset there are thousands more who will have timed their investments very badly and lost a lot of money.

Crypto enthusiasts like to say 'HODL' (Hold On for Dear Life), which they hope will ensure people don't panic and sell out of their position. The problem is that the evidence shows that all too many people find it very hard to do this. Far more people have panicked and sold out of their crypto holdings at a loss than have continued to hold. Or, perhaps they sold out at a 50% profit and missed out on another 5,000% since then. This also happens a great deal.

It is perhaps also worth mentioning that it is only in the crypto world where it is legally permissible for people to talk about and post about point-to-point price moves on social media to encourage you to invest. Because that sort of information is so fundamentally misleading, this is actually illegal in the world of regulated products like funds and shares, where there are very strict rules about how performance numbers are shown.

You can see the impact of volatility and the role played by human psychology in the crypto market from just how heavily correlated the volume of crypto commentary on social media is with price performance.

When the price is at historically *high* levels, you see huge numbers of people talking about it on social media and even crowing about how much money they've 'made'. But crypto fans go very quiet when the sector is down. This is the precise opposite of what would be ideal, at least if you want to make money.

This is a classic example of human psychology increasing the likelihood that we will buy high and sell low. All the noise about crypto when prices are high increases the risk that we suffer FOMO and buy at those levels, yet there are far fewer voices to reassure us when prices have plummeted, increasing the risk that we sell out in a panic.

The clear record of history is that, in the long run, it is hard to make money in very volatile assets purely because of how our brains work.

The second fundamental reason that crypto profits may prove elusive in the long run for many people is the extent to which these returns tend not to be based on any kind of *real* underlying economic activity. Most of the money made in crypto is zero-sum. If you have 'won' it is likely to be because other people have lost.

By contrast, as we've already seen throughout this book, the great thing about investment is that you can benefit from human progress and real economic growth. The ultimate reason stock markets go up over time is not because you're 'ripping someone else's face off', as a trader might say, but because of the development of the economy in terms of real, tangible things. We create economic value as a species by building buildings and factories, launching ships, selling tickets to concerts and football matches, developing new software, curing disease, and thousands of other similar things that generate a real, tangible, economic outcome – and *real* wealth.

This is completely different to 'making' hundreds or even thousands of percentage points in some kind of crypto investment – because more often than not there is unlikely to be any real economic progress that underpins that return. You will only have made thousands of percent because lots of other people have lost money.

A few of the leading crypto projects may have real value. Bitcoin may have a real role to play in the fullness of time as an alternative to the fiat currency system.[12] To a certain extent it already does. There are plenty of other projects in the crypto space which may have real-world value in time. It is highly likely, however, that most won't.

The development of the internet in the 1990s gives us a great example of this point. Lots of fans of crypto argue that crypto and blockchain will be 'just as big as the internet'. They'll create vast amounts of economic value; produce the next wave of success stories like Apple, Amazon, Facebook and Google; and make many people very wealthy in the process.

This is almost certainly true. Again, to a certain extent it is already true with the crypto industry being valued at around $3 trillion. But this doesn't mean that you will definitely pick the winners. The point here is that 'hindsight is 20/20'. It is easy to point to the handful of tech companies today that have been massive success stories. It was much more difficult, however, to pick those companies in the early days of the internet.

People investing in the dot-com boom in the late 1990s had a far higher chance of investing in companies that then went bust or saw their share prices fall a very long way, than in the tiny minority of companies that are now enormous household names. This is because there were far more of the former than the latter. This is what happens in investment, particularly when it comes to new technologies.

If you had been investing in 1999, in the early days of the development of the internet, how would you have known that Google

[12] 'Fiat' currency is money issued by governments – such as the dollar in the US or pound in the UK.

was the one to own rather than Excite, Lycos, America Online or Yahoo? Or that Apple, which was not yet in the mobile phone business, would end up dominating that market and destroying the huge and seemingly indestructible mobile phone giants of the day, like Nokia, Ericsson, Motorola and Siemens? Facebook was five years away from even existing in 1999.

The simple point here is that even if crypto is certainly an interesting, high-growth area, this does not mean that you have any guarantee of picking the 'right' investments in that space. Just as with any emerging technology, there will be more losers than winners, which makes the whole asset class very risky. For all we know, the overriding winner in the crypto space might not even exist yet.

That having been said, there is a chance that bitcoin itself is something of a special case. It has entered the mainstream in recent years and this trend looks set to continue. Bitcoin may end up playing a similar role to gold in time. To a certain extent it already is. For that reason, there may be merit in holding a small amount of your money in it.

If you want to hold at least some crypto to have exposure to the space overall, you will probably be best served by simply investing in bitcoin and ignoring all of the other crypto assets given how much uncertainty surrounds their future. There are more than 20,000 crypto coins in existence, and I don't think it is controversial to say that you should be very careful about almost all of them.

If you do decide to have some bitcoin, you must ensure that you spend a good amount of time learning how to buy and store it securely.

Crypto is basically unregulated

Another point to make about crypto generally is that it is largely unregulated and there have been a number of very high-profile crypto scandals over the years that have lost a lot of people a great deal of money. Perhaps the best known of these was the FTX scandal in November 2022. This was one of the largest cryptocurrency collapses in history.

FTX, once the second-largest crypto exchange in the world, filed for bankruptcy as a result of financial mismanagement and fraud. The collapse left more than one million customers nursing more than $8 billion of losses. The founder of FTX, Sam Bankman-Fried, faced multiple criminal charges and was sentenced to 25 years in prison. It was only the latest in a long line of crypto scandals and Ponzi schemes[13] that have lost investors tens of billions of dollars since crypto was invented. These have included:

- Mt. Gox – this was once the largest crypto exchange, but it was hacked in 2014 and investors lost around 850,000 bitcoins.
- Bitconnect – a Ponzi scheme that lost investors around $2.4 billion in 2018.
- OneCoin – another Ponzi scheme that lost people an estimated $4 billion in 2017.
- The Terra/Luna collapse – this one was even bigger than FTX, losing investors an estimated $60 billion in 2022![14]

There have been plenty of other, smaller scandals, many of which have still lost investors hundreds of millions.

A big part of the reason that there has been such huge interest in crypto, and why it is such a risky asset class, has to do with it being unregulated.

In most countries, there are very strict rules for anyone who wants to promote financial assets like shares or investment funds. To do that legally, people have to pass lots of exams to gain professional qualifications and prove they know what they're talking about.

This isn't the case for bitcoin and other crypto assets; the space is unique in this regard. Anyone can set themselves up as an 'expert' and make wild promises online about how you are 'guaranteed' to make 'life-changing' returns or 'thousands of percent a year'. If a finance professional working with regulated financial markets were to say such things, pretty quickly they could find themselves facing several years in prison!

---

[13] A Ponzi scheme (named after Charles Ponzi, who ran the first one in 1919) is a fraudulent investment scam where returns to earlier investors are paid using money from new investors, rather than from genuine profits. It relies on a constant flow of new money to survive, and once new investments dry up, the scheme collapses.

[14] https://www.forbes.com/sites/qai/2022/09/20/what-really-happened-to-luna-crypto/

All too many of the 'experts' in the crypto world have few if any financial qualifications or professional experience working in financial markets. Despite this, many of them have looked as though they knew what they were talking about, either because they were selling Ponzi schemes which had yet to collapse or simply because whilst the market goes up they look like they know what they're doing.

But this is something you must be very, very careful about. As Warren Buffett has said:

> Only when the tide goes out do you discover who has been swimming naked.[15]

The other problem with crypto being unregulated means that much of it can be a complete Wild West in terms of what people are actually buying. In the dot-com boom of the late 1990s, tech companies raising money were at least functioning within the constraints of a stock market – something that has operated within a strict legal structure for nearly two centuries. As leading investor Jim Rogers has put it:

> There have been plenty of bubbles I have seen in my life but this one is a little strange, because at least when the dot-com bubble was around, those were companies that said they had a business.[16]

During the dot-com boom, people may have taken complete leave of their senses in terms of what they were willing to pay for highly speculative early-stage companies that were losing lots of money, but at least those companies had been vetted by a raft of professionals in some shape or form and were actually doing something commercial, or trying to at least.

Even if a company like pets.com was a terrible business model, which haemorrhaged money on every bag of pet food it shipped,

---

[15] Cited in 'One of Warren Buffett's famous quotes is about to come true', *Fortune*, 3 October 2022, https://fortune.com/2022/10/03/warren-buffett-famous-quotes-swimming-naked-interest-rates-debt-zombies/. Last accessed 1 August 2025.

[16] Cited at https://x.com/TheStreet/status/946781376069689344. Last accessed 1 August 2025.

it was genuinely trying to sell pet food to customers via the internet. Its business plan and accounts had been looked over by bankers, financial analysts, accountants and auditors. Its various legal contracts had been verified by lawyers and it was not permitted to raise money from investors on the US stock market without sign-off from US regulatory bodies, which gave consideration to all of the above.

People have quite rightly criticized regulators on both sides of the Atlantic over their numerous failures in the dot-com boom and during the global financial crisis from 2008 onwards. There is no question that they have far from a perfect track record. That said, it isn't hard to argue that *some* regulation is better than none at all.

Despite those crashes and plenty of other high-profile company failures and scandals over the years, the system does actually function most of the time for thousands of perfectly sensible companies, in dozens of countries and across every sector of the economy. It has done for generations.

The same cannot be said of the crypto space. In the crypto world, people with entrepreneurial ideas looking to raise money have used a structure called an Initial Coin Offering, or ICO. Depending on what source you consider, there have been as many as 4,000 Initial Coin Offerings in the crypto space in the last few years, which have raised billions of dollars of real money. Research has found that nearly 60% of these have been scams of one kind or another![17]

To quote *Forbes* magazine:

> ...insider trading and dirty deals are flagrant. One coin-offering creator told Metastable Capital's Naval Ravikant, the CEO and cofounder of AngelList: 'If you agree to buy tokens at the ICO and support the price, then 30 days later, we'll secretly sell you any leftover tokens at a lower, pre-agreed price,' recalls Ravikant. That's a felony on Wall Street. In the cryptocurrency Wild West? 'These are the kinds of deals being cut left and right.'[18]

There are many more similar examples, and there are so many scams out there. Sadly, because these things are not regulated, people who

[17] https://blog.sagipl.com/ico-statistics/. Last acccessed 1 August 2025.

[18] https://www.forbesafrica.com/cover-story/2017/09/04/emperors-new-coins/. Last accessed 1 August 2025.

should be nowhere near these sorts of investments are investing their hard-earned money. Some are even buying crypto on credit cards or increasing their mortgage to get on board!

A related point here is that a big part of the reason for the extreme price movements in crypto assets in the last few years has been the extraordinary role played by social media. The dot-com boom happened at a time when social media didn't exist and even email as a marketing technology was in its infancy.

Things are completely different today. Never before in history has it been possible for such a relatively large proportion of the world's population to get excited about an investment. Between them, the Meta Platform's main apps – Facebook, Instagram, Messenger and WhatsApp – have nearly 4 billion active monthly users.

This is unprecedented and means that 'the madness of crowds' can and has been stronger for bitcoin and crypto than for any other financial asset in history. Never before have so many people with no knowledge of financial markets been sold a financial product in the way they have in the last few years. All too often the people selling them the product have no knowledge of financial markets either!

Vast numbers of people have 'invested' for the worst reason of all – because they see the price going up and they see other people 'making money'.

The problem with that is that this effect can be just as powerful on the way down as it was on the way up, as everyone panics and sees those around them start to lose money. The fact that the bitcoin price has done extraordinarily well up to the time of writing doesn't change any of the points made over the last few pages, particularly the ones about human psychology. It will be entirely possible for the bitcoin price to continue to rise but for lots of people to lose money nevertheless!

There are plenty of other challenges with crypto. It's very hard to value using conventional valuation techniques, for example. As we saw a few pages back, the way we value a company listed on the stock market is to look at things like its revenues, profits and assets. This is basically impossible to do with crypto assets.

Trading crypto can also create a real headache for you when it comes to how it is taxed – something a lot of young or inexperienced crypto traders have failed to understand. If you make money buying and selling financial assets, you will owe the government capital gains tax. Many people involved in crypto have a huge administrative headache ahead of them, if they have made dozens or even hundreds of trades over the years, and failed to keep accurate records. They might owe the government a lot of money. Remember that the penalty for getting such things wrong can be big fines or, worse, time in prison!

In summary

Crypto assets and blockchain technology are certainly an interesting area but it is very important to understand the various points we've made over the last few pages. If you are excited by the possibilities of crypto assets, by all means consider making an investment but realize that this will be highly speculative and risky.

This is fine for, say, 1–5% of your investible capital, maybe 10% if you're particularly keen and willing to do the work required to really understand what you're doing.

I would come back to a common theme that repeats throughout the book that, over a lifetime of investment, the investment tortoise generally does a great deal better than the investment hare. There are two centuries of evidence to that effect.

You don't need to chase an asset that might offer you a 'once in a generation' opportunity to 'get rich quick' to do a perfectly good job at building wealth.

To conclude…

Having read this chapter, you should now feel pretty confident about your understanding of the main financial products that exist. You do not need to have an extremely detailed understanding of all of these things, but a basic grasp should be pretty helpful.

Now you have that basic grasp, it's time to look in more detail at some of the concrete steps you will want to take to get your finances humming.

9
The accounts you will need

If you have read thus far, you will hopefully have worked out how to find some money for saving and investment. Before we go on to look at some of the specifics around how to get that money to work, the first thing we should cover is the key financial *accounts* that you are going to need.

Wherever you are in the world there are basically three of these:

1 A 'checking', 'current', 'transaction' or 'everyday' account
2 A pension account of some kind
3 An investment account of some kind, over and above your pension.

So, let's look at each of these in turn...

1 A 'checking', 'current', 'transaction' or 'everyday' account

This is your main bank account administratively. Your wage or salary will be paid into it, usually automatically, and most of your bills will be paid out of it. It is also where you're most likely to keep any cash you need to cover things you need to pay for in the short term.

In the US, these are called 'checking accounts' and in Canada 'chequing accounts'. In the UK, they tend to be called 'current accounts', and in Australia and New Zealand they're usually called 'transaction' or 'everyday' accounts.

Wherever you are in the world, it is pretty important to have one of these. Most of us in the developed world open one at some point in our teens. These accounts help you keep your money safe, as your cash is protected by the bank. They're also usually insured by a government agency of some kind, such as the FDIC in the US and FSCS in the UK.

Checking or current accounts enable you to make lots of key payments automatically, which is far less hassle than managing everything yourself. You can also make bank transfers to other people or businesses. Most banks will provide you with a debit card for online and in-store purchases and for withdrawing cash from a network of ATMs. These days, many banks also offer financial tracking and budgeting apps, and various perks such as free or discounted travel insurance, car breakdown cover, or discounts on certain other products and services, particularly for younger customers and students.

Your credit score

Arguably the most important point about these accounts is that you need one to build up a financial history. This is critical for something called your 'creditworthiness' and for your credit score.

A credit score is a numerical rating that rates your creditworthiness based on how you use your bank account and other financial services over time. This is vital when it comes to using any kind of credit or debt product such as a credit card, loan or mortgage. Lenders of all kinds will use your credit score to work out the risk of lending you money.

A higher credit score will mean you can borrow more money, at lower interest rates, with lower fees and better terms. A low score can result in higher costs and interest rates. If you have a really bad credit score you may not be able to borrow any money at all. Credit scores are influenced by things like your payment history, how you have used any credit or debt in the past, how long your credit history is and so on. This is why it is a good idea to get a checking or current account as soon as you can, to help you build the highest credit score you can. This could save you huge amounts of money over the years on any debt you might want to use.

Please also remember the points I made about credit and debt earlier in the book in Chapter 7, in particular how important it is to be very careful about how you use such things.

Whilst it is important and useful to have one of these accounts, it is also important to use them properly. Few of them pay you much, if any interest on any cash you keep in the account. There can be fees and charges too, which you should watch out for.

The main idea with such accounts, therefore, is to keep as little money in them as possible. You should have a clear idea of what you need to live on each month, and how much is coming into the account and going out of it. Add a little buffer or margin for error, and then ensure that any surplus cash coming into that account is *automatically* paid out every month into accounts that will enable you to make the most of your money.

2 A pension account of some kind

The next big account most people should make sure they think about and get right is a *pension* account of some kind. It is a well-known fact that most people find the whole idea of pensions very boring. This is a big problem, because it means that many millions of people all over the world are failing to make the most of their pension arrangements. Neglecting them can mean a great deal of stress and unhappiness later in life.

Leading British finance writer Iona Bain has suggested that pensions need a rebrand. She thinks we would all be better off if we called them 'Future Funds' instead; I agree!

Getting your pension arrangements right as soon as you can, and putting them on autopilot, can and will make a huge difference to your financial prospects and to your ability to become wealthy. So, please don't think of them as boring and definitely don't be a proverbial ostrich and stick your head in the sand and ignore them for years – as far, far too many people do!

Pensions are in fact far from boring, for two main reasons:

1 The technology of a pension has enabled hundreds of millions of people throughout history to stop working completely at a certain point in their lives and have enough money to live on for many years thereafter, sometimes even decades. That is surely far from boring! It is actually a pretty amazing thing, and it is worth highlighting that comfortably 99% of human beings in our species' history didn't get to enjoy this outcome. For most of human history, people generally had to work until they died. When you really think about it, the invention of the pension is something we should all be very grateful for!

2 The trillions of dollars, pounds, euros, yen and so on in pension funds all over the world are used to fund things. They provide the capital that enables us to pay for so many of the things that are good in this world, including the homes and offices we live and work in, the food we eat, football stadiums, planes, cars, trucks, ships, the fashion and beauty industries, movies and TV shows and video games. All of that is also far from boring, surely?

One of the reasons so many people are so disengaged from the whole idea of a pension has to do – once again – with human psychology. Research shows that we think of our future selves as complete strangers, as weird as that might sound. As a result, we aren't that interested in sacrificing a certain amount of money today to make sure that our 'stranger' future selves have a better life. This is a well-understood reality.

It is very important to fight this, however. If you don't, you will be at risk of being pretty poor when you are older. Remember, very few governments are going to be able to pay you a decent income in retirement because of how long everyone is living nowadays and how many more old people there will be in the future, as compared to younger workers paying tax.

That is the 'stick', if you like. If you don't sort this out now, you could have a pretty tough future. More happily, the 'carrot' is that if you do, you can make a huge difference to your future relatively easily and very significantly increase the chance you become wealthy, particularly if you start young! One of the key benefits of investing in your pension is that there tend to be significant tax advantages in doing so, which can turbo-charge your ability to build wealth.

The other key point is that it really isn't that hard and doesn't have to be much of a sacrifice either. Doing the work required to get things set and putting a little money into a pension as soon as you can is a small price to pay given the huge benefits that should result.

With a little bit of time and effort now, you should make a six- or even seven-figure difference to your future. Your future self will thank you, as will any dependents you might have by the time you get there.

There are basically three broad kinds of pensions:

1 A pension from the government

In most parts of the world you are likely to get a pension of some kind from the government. What this looks like and how it works will depend on where you live. In the US, the pension system is known as Social Security. In the UK, it is called the State Pension.

It is very important to understand that in most developed world pension systems, the government only provides a very basic level of income that is usually not enough to support the lifestyle that most people want. You will also have to pay into the system for many years to make sure you are entitled to your pension when the time comes. In the US, your social security payments will be based on your highest 35 years of earnings. Similarly, in the UK you have to pay into the system for 35 years to get the maximum amount available.

As we have seen, most countries are also confronting something of a crisis in their pension systems as a result of aging populations, longer life expectancies, and shrinking workforces. This may result in pension incomes being reduced during your lifetime, or only becoming available to you when you're older than is the case today.

Given this reality and given that you will get relatively little money from the government anyway, almost no matter where you live, you need to ensure you make the most of your other pension arrangements. This brings us to the other two kinds of pension.

2 A pension provided by your employer

Arguably the most important pension for most people will be one provided by their employer.

The most common of these in the US is called a 401(k) plan. In the UK, such things tend to be called 'workplace' or 'occupational' pensions. These are schemes that are set up by the company you work for.

In most countries, it is fairly common for any company you work for to provide you with a pension of some kind. In many countries companies are actually forced to do this by law. Many employers, particularly bigger companies, will also invest money in your account for you or match any contributions you make to your pension yourself. If you decide to put 100 dollars or pounds into your pension each month, they will add another 100.

The other key point to make here is that in most pension systems you can put money into your pension from your *pre-tax* income. This is essentially some free extra money from the government to encourage you to save and invest and a really big advantage of a pension generally.

The fact that you can get a fair bit of free money from your employer and from the government is great news for your ability to build wealth, and a big part of the reason why it really is worth getting to grips with your pension as soon as you can. The more years you spend getting free money, the better – as should be clear!

3 A 'private' pension that you arrange yourself

Most people should be reasonably well-served by the combination of a small pension from the government and a bigger one arranged and funded by your various employers over a lifetime of working.

There is, however, a third category of pension to be aware of: a private pension that you arrange yourself, or pay a financial adviser to arrange.

This kind of pension is of particular relevance to anyone who is self-employed. In recent years there has been a huge rise in people working in what is called the 'gig economy'. That is to say that there are millions more people working part-time or as freelancers, and fewer full-time jobs than there were in the past. Working as a freelancer or part-time can have its merits, particularly in terms of flexibility. You can work when you want to work and even live somewhere exciting. There are plenty of 'digital nomads' nowadays who are able to live and work anywhere that has a decent internet connection.

Whilst this can be very good fun and a great life, if you are self-employed, you will have to make your own pension arrangements. Happily, it is usually possible to do this. In the US, you can contribute to something called an 'Individual Retirement Account' or IRA for short. In the UK there is something called a 'Self-Invested Private Pension' or SIPP, and there are similar systems around the world. The basic point is that there will usually be some kind of pension account that gives you tax benefits if you use it to build wealth for your future.

Private pensions are particularly useful, then, if you are self-employed, but they have other uses and potential advantages. Some wealthy people take advantage of a private pension in addition to what they have with their employer, for example, as this can mean they can save and invest more than they might be able to do in their employer's scheme. Private pensions can also give you more flexibility about what to invest in than many workplace or occupational pensions. They can also be useful if you're the sort of person who changes jobs quite regularly. Many systems permit you to have your own private pension account and then have your employer make contributions to that account rather than insist you join the company pension scheme.

Access to your money

Another key consideration that is important to bear in mind here is that in most pension systems you will not be able to access any money that goes into your pension account(s) until you reach a certain age. In the US, the earliest someone can access their 401(k) without incurring any penalty is 59 and a half years old (which is weird but that's the law). In the UK, you can't access pension money until the 'normal minimum pension age', which is 55 at the time of writing. This number is also due to increase to 57 in April 2028 and could well increase still further in the years ahead given the state of the British economy and pension system.

This aspect of pension investment is clearly good news for maximizing the chance that you will actually have enough to live on by the time you wish to retire, because you can't raid the piggy bank along the way, but it is important to bear this in mind as you decide how to allocate whatever you can afford to save and invest each month. You need to be happy that any money you allocate will be locked up until you hit retirement age, which will be many years in the future for most readers of this book.

As you might already be able to tell, pensions can be quite complicated. There are quite a few things to think about and get straight, including the tax benefits and potential contributions from your employer. Although this all sounds quite complicated, it is well worth taking the time to arrange things as best you can, and as early as you can, given the huge potential upside in doing so.

If you are employed, it's a good idea to speak to the relevant person at your company to make sure you understand what your options are with regard to your pension. You will also want to ensure your pension money is doing the best it can for you in terms of how it is being invested – something you will hopefully be better placed to do once you've read the rest of this book.

If you are self-employed, it is probably a good idea to speak to a financial adviser about such things. We have already looked at the fact that such personalized investment advice can be quite expensive, but if you're self-employed and want to get this important stuff right, you may want to bite the bullet at some point and seek professional advice.

The alternative is to learn enough about such things so that you can work it all out yourself. Or, you could ask for help from your parents, another relative, or a qualified friend. Just make sure that anyone you do end up asking really does know what they're talking about! This will save you the cost of getting professional advice, even if it does take a bit of time and effort on your part. What you decide to do will be a personal choice.

It is worth highlighting that getting this stuff right is a marathon, not a sprint. The key thing is to get to grips with the basics and aim to get things set up and running as smoothly as possible as soon as you can. If you work for a big company, they should be able to set you on the right path. You have the whole of your working life to tweak, hone and improve such things as you go along, but the key thing is to do something to ensure you are building wealth – as soon as possible.

The final point to make is that, although these considerations are relatively complicated, what follows in the rest of this book should help you formulate your thoughts. The last section of the book provides a framework for thinking about investment overall. Once you've read it, you will hopefully have a better idea of how to get things roughly right, and that should get you a fair way down the road to optimizing your investments over time. Just get started, so you don't leave those employer contributions and tax benefits on the table!

3 An investment account of some kind, over and above your pension

The last of the main three accounts you will want to use in your life to grow wealth is an investment account of some kind. In many parts of the world there are tax-efficient accounts you can use here too. In the US there is something called a 'Roth IRA', which can offer tax benefits if you invest in the account for long enough. In the UK there is something called a 'Stocks and Shares ISA' (ISA stands for 'Individual Savings Account').

These sorts of accounts and their counterparts in other countries can give you access to thousands of different investments, including funds, stocks and shares, ETFs and so on. In an ideal world, you will want to start putting some money to work in an investment account each month, in addition to whatever you are doing with your pension arrangements, if at all possible.

So now we've looked at the three key accounts you need to set you up for financial stability and maximize your chances of becoming wealthy. In the third and final section of the book we'll look in more detail at how to put all of this into practice.

PART III

Getting an amazing result

- Investing vs trading
- Four key ideas:
    - Investing for the long run
    - Investing regularly each month – automating
    - Ignoring the news and sticking to your guns
    - Using the idea of '100 minus your age'
- Bringing it all together

10

Investing vs trading

In the first two sections of the book we have covered:

- How important money and financial markets are for all of us
- Why you can and should learn about money and finance
- Two amazing facts about finance
- Two crucial investment themes
- How to find the money for savings and investment
- Key steps to take before you begin to invest
- The key asset classes
- The three main accounts you need.

Now it's time to bring it all together and look at how you can increase the chance that you get an amazing result for your money in the years ahead.

Investing vs trading

Once you understand the basic asset classes, have eradicated any expensive debt and saved a decent amount of cash in your 'rainy day' pot, you are ready to start investing.

It is very important to stress here, however, that I am talking about *investing*, not *trading*. These are two very different things! One of the most important things to understand when it comes to your finances and maximizing the chance that you become wealthy is the crucial difference between investing and trading.

This is a topic that is incredibly poorly understood, and never more so than today with the rise of social media, the crypto market, and far too many Instagram and TikTok influencers who have never passed a finance exam dishing out financial advice online.

It is really important to understand the extent to which trading and investing are two completely different things. Failing to understand this difference is one of the key reasons so many people fail with their finances – and can fall victim to scammers and con artists, too.

First of all, investing is for absolutely *everyone* – almost no matter how much you earn. It is something everyone should start doing as soon as they are able to, even with tiny amounts of money, and keep on doing for their entire working life, no matter what is going on with the news or the economy.

The same cannot be said about trading. At the most basic level, the reason this is so important is quite simply because for the significant majority of people:

- You have a high chance of making money and becoming wealthy if you invest.
- You have a high chance of losing money if you trade.

To be clear, there is nothing inherently wrong with trading. Done well and done at the right time in your life and under the right conditions, it can be powerful, and potentially a good way to grow your wealth. But investing really should be everyone's first priority.

This is because investing is about gradually building wealth over a long period of time. You invest whatever you can afford into something sensible every month for many years. If you do this reasonably well over a long period of time, you have a solid chance of becoming wealthy – no matter your income, background, or education level.

There is more than a century of evidence that this is the case. It is how the majority of millionaires became millionaires. Investing works because it gives you financial exposure to human progress. This is something tangible and real.

Trading, on the other hand, refers to the frequent buying and selling of stocks, currencies, commodities or other financial instruments with the aim of making short-term profits. Unlike long-term investing, which focuses on steady wealth accumulation over years or decades, trading relies on attempting to predict short-term price movements in financial markets, often over days, hours, or even minutes, and requires a great deal more skill than investing.

Investing is about human progress and global growth. It provides capital for real businesses that are doing real things in the real economy. Trading is much more of a zero-sum game. It's essentially financial speculation, which doesn't really create anything. If you win, it is generally because someone else has lost. This means that while investing is fundamentally good for the world and for human flourishing, the same can't always be said about trading.

To be clear, some people *can* make a great deal of money through trading, but it is really important to understand that most people don't. In fact, 70–80% of people lose money when trading.

The reason for this is actually quite simple: becoming a good trader is hard and time-consuming.

If you are going to trade, you really must learn the skills required to do it well. There is a great deal of work required to become a half-decent trader. To do it properly so that you have enough skill to stay safe when you do it is probably not far off the work required to get a degree from a university – before you will get properly comfortable and consistently good and have the deep understanding of financial markets and the key trading techniques you will need. Even then, there is no guarantee you will get there, even if you are willing to do the work.

It is worth thinking about the fact that, to be good enough, you will need to understand the subject matter really well. Ideally, you will need to be an A-grade student or close to it. If you have a poor understanding of what is certainly a complicated subject, there is a real risk that you will lose money.

Just as you wouldn't want an airline pilot or brain surgeon who had only a mediocre understanding of their subject matter, you really don't want to be a trader unless you have a very firm grasp of what you're doing. This idea should come sharply into focus when you consider that you will be competing with some of the smartest and best-resourced people in the world if you do decide to start trading.

Moreover, even if you are willing to put in all of this work to learn about trading, the amount of time and effort required to actually do it successfully on an ongoing basis is significant, and prohibitively so for many people. This is certainly the case if you're a busy parent, or if you're just starting out in your career and have a tonne of work and study to do. You should be careful about anyone who tells you it 'only takes five minutes a day'. It might take them five minutes a day after years of practice, but that will absolutely not be true for you as a beginner (not if you want to do it properly and avoid losing money).

Also, if you're going to take the very real risk of losing the money that you've worked so hard to earn and save, shouldn't you be spending more than five minutes a day on it anyway? This is pretty important stuff, after all.

Another really crucial point that is poorly understood is the fact that unless you have significant net worth available to you as liquid assets and cash, trading is actually highly likely to be something of a waste of your time in *absolute* terms.

The financial return you might make on the time you spend trading will be fairly small compared to lots of other things you might be doing with that time. Unless you have quite a lot of money already, ideally a chunky five- or even six-figure sum, you are not going to be able to get enough money to work at a low enough risk to make all that extra work and time spent staring at screens worthwhile - in absolute terms.

The best trading educators will show you that you should only ever risk a relatively small amount of your money on each trade, ideally not more than 1%. If you follow that advice, as you almost certainly should, and you only have a few hundred or even a few thousand dollars to work with, then you'll only be able to make relatively small amounts of money from trading.

If you think about this in terms of the optimal return on your *time* (which is by far your most valuable resource), this is likely to be pretty poor compared to many other things you could be doing with that time.

Say for example, you have even as much as £10,000 to trade. Even if you have a fantastic year and make a 30% or 40% annual return, you will only have made £3,000 or £4,000 in absolute terms over the course of a year. Although this might sound great, for a beginner this will likely have required many, many hours of your time to achieve.

It's important to think quite deeply about whether that time might have been better spent doing something else. If you'd spent those hours on getting better at your job, or even on getting a new job, might you have managed to increase your salary by a great deal more than that? For many people this is possible, in time at least.

An increase in your skill level or salary also has the advantage that you're very likely to benefit from that increase for many years to come. In contrast, for many new traders a 30% or 40% year will often be followed by a year where you lose money, which is nowhere near as good an outcome, clearly.

Let's put it another way: the return on trading is far less *reliable* than the return on becoming more skilled and better paid. The hours you spend trying to learn how to trade currencies or glued to crypto groups on social media would almost certainly be better spent becoming better and more valuable at your day job, and getting paid more as a result. Or, if you hate your day-job, on spending the time to figure out what else you could do with your life, acquiring the skills to do it and making that move.

All too often, people who have very little money go straight to things like crypto and currency trading, completely bypassing doing their best with far more fundamental things like saving, investing and doing the best with their pension. This is doing things in the wrong order. You might think about this as being like someone with a white belt in karate or judo fighting black belts on day one of their martial arts journey; very likely to result in you getting hurt.

It's also important to note that trading and crypto services tend to be expensive precisely because they promise 'life-changing returns'. One of the worst rookie mistakes you can make is to be someone with, say, \$3,000 of savings paying some unregulated 'guru' \$1,000 or even more of that to 'learn trading'. Many decades of evidence shows that most people will be better off spending their time on things that earn them money and saving and investing (not trading) 10% or more of those earnings for many years until they have much, much more than a few thousand dollars or pounds.

People fail at trading for all of these reasons and more. It really is a completely inappropriate activity for the vast majority of people. Even the best trading educators, whilst sometimes teaching viable skills, often don't actually help people improve their finances in the real world. When you consider the high percentage of people who lose money trading, the evidence shows that simple, regular investing into a sensible mix of funds is likely to be a much better idea.

This is also a set-and-forget approach to success, which really only needs to be looked at every five or even ten years to have a massively positive impact on your chances of becoming wealthy. This kind of approach to *investing* is the focus of the rest of this book.

To be clear, I am not saying that all trading is bad or that everyone working in the field is unethical. If you have the time and the money and are ready to do the work, then learning how to trade is something to consider.

It is just that this is only something you should do *after* you have put the more fundamental financial building blocks in place, and after you have built up enough of a capital base to make it worthwhile. Even then, you should only get into it if you are willing to commit a great deal of time and effort.

Sadly, too many people are trading when they really would be far better off investing. If this sounds horribly boring, it is probably worth bearing in mind that the best investors and the most successful people think in terms of decades, not months or years.

If you want to maximize the probability that you become wealthy later in life, two of your greatest allies are time and patience. When you become sufficiently wealthy – let's say in your thirties, forties, or fifties, depending on how early you start and how much you earn – that is the time that you might deploy some (not all!) of that wealth into trading, single stock investment or crypto.

One of the most important ideas for succeeding in life generally is deploying the 80/20 rule to all that you do. That is to say that you should focus 80% of your effort on the 20% of actions that bring you 80% of your success. For many people, trading is just not a good use of their time, in absolute terms.

For most people, perhaps the best time to become a trader is once they are retired. If you have a fair bit of money, a decent amount of time on your hands and an interest in financial markets, this could be a great activity for you. For much of the rest of the population, however, it really isn't, particularly for younger people and busy parents.

Tragically, many people try *trading* and lose money and then give up on *investment* – because they fail to understand that these are two completely different things.

Investing

Now that we understand the key difference between investing and trading, let's look in more detail at investing.

Investment success is probably about 90% admin and only 10% asset selection.

This is certainly not a scientific number. The point is that if you establish the right saving and investment habits, channel your money into the right accounts and invest in almost anything vaguely sensible for many years, there is a high chance that you will make some exceptional forward progress with your money. You could very likely become a millionaire if you do this consistently for a long enough period of time, almost no matter what you earn.

The vast majority of people simply don't do this. Often this is because they don't have enough confidence about what a 'sensible' approach to their finances might be, so they do nothing, like the proverbial 'rabbit in the headlights'. Or, they don't understand compounding, so they don't have any sense of what is possible. This is nothing short of tragic for tens, or even hundreds of millions of people and, perhaps even more importantly, for the societies we live in.

Over the next few pages, we're going to look at a logical approach to investment that anyone can understand and implement, and that should help you get past this block.

As a key first step on that road, it is worth revisiting the big-picture end goal of investment. The clearer an idea you have of where you want to go, the more likely you are to succeed in getting there.

The whole point of investment is that there comes a magical moment at some stage in your life when you are able to live on your money – or, even better, the money you make from your money – rather than the money you make from working.

In the language of economics: you are able to live on your capital rather than from your labour. This should be everyone's north star when they think about investment and financial markets.

If this sounds crazily unrealistic to you, then I would point out that this is the whole idea of a pension.

Of course, you may also want to use investment to help you achieve certain financial goals long before retirement. This would include short- to medium-term things like saving for a holiday, or a large expense such as a car, a wedding or a deposit on a property.

Using financial market investment to grow your money can potentially help you achieve such things more quickly than the traditional approach of saving only in cash. That said, it is crucial to strike the right balance between chasing higher returns and taking on the risks that are inherent in financial markets – a key focus of this section of the book.

If you start early enough and do a sufficiently good job with investment, you could even find yourself able to live on your money some way earlier than traditional retirement age. We already looked at the FIRE movement earlier in the book. If you can get to a large six- or even seven-figure investment pot, you may be able to live on your money, rather than on what you earn from working, much earlier in your life than many people think possible.

Or, you will be able to continue to work and supplement your income from your investments, meaning that you'll have more freedom to do something you love or to leave a job if you don't like it. Hopefully this is quite a nice thought!

Many people think the idea of getting to a large six- or even seven-figure sum is unrealistic. We have already showed that this is not the case, because of the power of compounding. Even people on average incomes can realistically aspire to achieve this if they do a sufficiently good job with investment over a long enough period of time. We will look at this in more detail in the pages that follow.

A big part of the reason so many people are cynical about this possibility is because they don't understand the power of compounding returns. As we saw earlier in the book, a majority of US and British adults don't understand compounding.

You might argue that this is one of the reasons so few people invest. Perhaps one of the other main reasons is because, when they think about investment, the first thing many people think about is the risk of a 'stock market crash'. So, let's deal with that concern first.

'How to invest so that crashes don't matter'

In December 2017 I was honoured to be asked to contribute a chapter to the prestigious *Harriman's New Book of Investing Rules* alongside some of the world's most famous investment professionals.

My guest chapter was called 'How to Invest So that Crashes Don't Matter'. As I said at the beginning of that piece:

> I believe that I can arrange my financial affairs such that I am comfortable that whether there is a massive crash or whether stock markets power ahead, my ability to meet my longer-run financial goals will be largely unaffected. You should feel the same way too.[1]

How can you be confident you can invest without worrying about financial markets crashing? How is this possible? In this section of the book, we are going to look at a number of key ideas that explain how.

One of the first things to understand when thinking about how to approach long-term saving and investing is that there are two key investment phases in your life. These are accumulation and decumulation (which is sometimes called 'drawdown'). Let's look at each of these in turn:

Accumulation

This is the period of your life in which you attempt to build wealth by saving and investing. You can think about this being your focus from roughly the age of 30 (or, ideally, younger) to the age of 60 (or younger, if possible).

What is really key here is that you must think in terms of this taking many years. For most people accumulation will take anywhere from 20 to 40 years. It is really important not to be in a hurry.

As we've already seen earlier in the book, time and a long-run approach are two of your biggest allies in investment, for all sorts of reasons. First, because you benefit from the incredible power of compounding for longer, and also because investing over the very long run helps you navigate volatility in financial markets. The longer your investment timeframe, the less you have to worry about financial market crashes. We will look at this in more detail shortly.

[1] Andrew Craig, 'How to invest so that crashes don't matter', in *Harriman's New Book of Investing Rules*, ed. Christopher Parker. Harriman House, 2017.

This is also why the earlier you start, the better – even if only with relatively small amounts of money.

Decumulation

The other key investment phase you need to understand is decumulation or 'drawdown'. This is the period in your life when you will want to live on the wealth you have built in the accumulation phase. We might think about this as roughly from age 60 onwards – or younger if you start early enough, can earn and invest a lot, or are particularly skilful and lucky with your investment returns.

As we've seen, the holy grail of investment is to get to the point where you can afford to live on the returns you make on your money. The standard assumption is that you can do this if your pot is something like 25 times your annual living expenses.

Risk of loss

Your focus needs to be on how you can do the best job you can with investment in both phases – accumulation and decumulation. There are two important considerations to keep in mind here:

1. Your *investment returns*. The higher these are, the more wealth you can build and the faster you can build it. You might think about this as the return *on* your money.
2. Avoiding loss. Obviously, you want to avoid suffering a large loss along the way. You can think of this as the return *of* your money!

One of the key challenges here is that investments which increase your chance of making a higher return generally also increase your chance of suffering a large loss.

Another important thing to consider is that a very large loss will impact you differently depending on how old you are. Not losing money becomes increasingly important as we get older.

The reasons for this should be fairly obvious: if you are 30 and have built an investment pot of, say, $10,000, a 50% stock market (or bitcoin) crash would reduce the value of that pot to around $5,000.

This isn't great, but it is clearly a lot less problematic and stressful than if you are 65 years old and the $1 million you have spent a lifetime building falls to $500,000 with the same percentage fall.

If you are 30 in this scenario, you still have many years ahead of you to grow your investment pot. If you are 65, however, you do not have that time and will more than likely need this money to fund you and your family in retirement.

This is why, for most people, the older you get, the more catastrophic a large loss is likely to be and the more you need to be thinking about the return *of* your money rather than your return *on* it.

What you want to do then is maximize your potential annualized investment returns over a lifetime of investing and minimize your risk of loss, especially as you get closer to retirement.

There are two key reasons why reducing the possibility of suffering a large loss is a very important consideration for an investor generally:

1 The crucial role played by human psychology
2 Something called 'the break-even fallacy'.

Let's look at each of these in turn.

1 Human psychology – we are hard-wired for failure

As we saw earlier in the book, we human beings are quite literally hard-wired psychologically to be bad investors. The way our brains work hugely increases the likelihood that we will buy high and sell low.

When we see an asset going up and 'lots of people making money', there is a high chance we will rush to buy that asset given how strong our FOMO (Fear of Missing Out) is. When we see that same asset plummet in value, there is an even higher chance we will panic and rush to sell it. Sadly, this is just human nature.

It is this panic selling that is of most concern when it comes to long-run stock market investment. Many higher-risk assets, like shares, *will* deliver high percentage returns in the long run. The problem is that they can be highly volatile over the course of that long run (they can go up and down a lot along the way). Few people are mentally tough enough to continue to own and continue to buy something that has fallen a long way – and this will always happen with riskier assets at various points in time.[2]

The record of many decades of evidence is that investing in the stock market will give you a good chance of making reasonably high real returns over time. At the same time, stock markets have a habit of crashing every few years, often by as much as 50% or more.

In the 2007-9 global financial crisis, for example, stock markets all over the world plunged. The S&P 500, which is arguably the world's most important index, fell from around 1,500 in October 2007 to the slightly spooky and biblical low of 666[3] by March 2009. That is a fall of around 56%. The British stock market fell by even more than this, as did pretty much every other stock market in the world to a greater or lesser extent. Each of these markets had done a very similar thing only a few years earlier in the dot-com sell-off of 2000–2002.

All over the world journalists wrote thousands of scary pieces about how 'dangerous' investment is and people reacted as they so often do when there is a stock market crash: they pulled money out of the stock market in a panic and gave up on investment. By doing this, they turned a theoretical loss into a real one.

At the time of writing, the S&P 500 is at around 6,000 – roughly 800% up from that 2009 low. People who gave up on stock market investment in recent years have potentially missed out in a big, life-changing way. Sad though this is, many people find it almost impossible to sit on a paper loss of any magnitude and ride it out, confident that things will get better in the longer term.

This is why stock market crashes can be so damaging, and many people are scared of the whole idea of investment. It seems too frightening and risky. But it really need not be, as we shall see below.

Financial products are one of the few things that people tend to buy when they're expensive and sell when they're cheap – for reasons of deep-seated human psychology. It is for this reason that most people's investment returns are generally a long way lower than the returns of

---

[2] A very good book on this subject is *The Psychology of Money* by Morgan Housel.

[3] This number is called 'the mark of the beast' in the Book of Revelation in the Bible. Hence the 'spooky' comment.

the stock market as a whole. And that is the people who are actually investing. Even worse, most people don't invest in the stock market at all so have no chance of benefiting from these sorts of returns, one of the main reasons so many people struggle financially. In the pages that follow we look at how you might deal with this reality.

2 The break-even fallacy

The fact that our brain can lead us to buy high, sell low and very possibly give up on investment entirely is bad enough, but there is actually something else in play that can make the impact of risk and volatility on your real-life ability to make money even worse! This is something called 'the break-even fallacy', which the evidence shows relatively few people understand.

The break-even fallacy is all about how mathematics works at the most fundamental level when it comes to calculating percentage returns. It is the fact that *a higher percentage return is required to get back from a price level to break-even (square one / where you started) than was suffered when an asset originally fell to that price level.*

If this sounds a bit complicated, hopefully the table below will make it clearer. As you can see from the table, if something you own falls 50% in price, you will then need it to go up 100% (not 50%) to get back to where you started. The phenomenon shown in this table is often poorly understood.

Many people naturally assume that if you lose 50% of your money, you will then need to gain 50% to get back to square one. This is incorrect. If you are down 50%, you will need to make fully 100% to recover that loss.

If you are down 25%, you will need to make 33%. If you suffer a 90% loss, you will need that thing to go back up 900%. At 95% down, you'll need to be lucky enough to see no less than a 1,900% recovery (as so many people have experienced in recent years with various 'altcoins' in the crypto world).

It is extremely important to understand this. If you have, say, 10,000 dollars or pounds in a higher-risk asset such as shares or bitcoin and you are unlucky enough to see a 50% fall in the value of your position (as people so often do in crashes), you will end up with 5,000. To

TABLE 1 An illustration of the break-even fallacy

Percentage loss	Percentage needed to recover loss	Percentage loss	Percentage needed to recover loss
5%	5.3%	50%	100.0%
10%	11.1%	55%	122.2%
15%	17.6%	60%	150.0%
20%	25.0%	65%	185.7%
25%	33.3%	70%	233.3%
30%	42.9%	75%	300.0%
35%	53.8%	80%	400.0%
40%	66.7%	85%	566.7%
45%	81.8%	90%	900.0%
		95%	**1900.0%**

get back to your original 10,000, you will then need to make a *100% return, not* a 50% return. This is a long road back.

This is why Warren Buffett, arguably the world's greatest living investor, has said:

> Rule No. 1: Never lose money. Rule No. 2: Never forget rule No. 1.

'A rock and a hard place...'

Throughout this book we have seen how important it is to maximize your chances of building wealth, particularly because you're not likely to get much from the government in the years ahead, no matter where you live. We have also shown the impact of crashes and the tough mathematics of the break-even fallacy.

It seems that we are stuck between the 'rock' of needing to make the highest investment returns we can and 'the hard place' of avoiding a significant loss at any point in our investment journey, especially as we approach retirement. Happily, there are ways you can deal with this reality. In the next chapter we will look at four of these.

11

Four key investing ideas

Over the next few pages, we are going to look at four crucial ideas that can help you maximize the chances that you get a great result with investing, minimize the risk that you lose money and, hopefully, give you real peace of mind along the way. These four key ideas are:

1. Investing for the long run, ideally the *very* long run
2. Investing regularly each month and automating your investments
3. Ignoring the news and sticking to your guns
4. Using an elegant approach to investment called '100 minus your age'.

Let's look at each in turn...

1 Invest for the long run, ideally the VERY long run

When it comes to investment, the clear evidence of history is that the longer you invest, the less likely you are to make a loss and the more likely you are to make a decent return. When it comes to shares, for example, several decades of evidence shows that if you invest in a stock market for one day you have roughly a 50% chance of making a positive return. If you invest for three months, this probability increases to around 65%. Investing for a year or more gives you about a 73% chance of being up. After ten years or so your chances increase to more than 94% and trend towards 100% in the years that follow.[1] These probabilities increase if you invest regularly each month – more on that below.

In the short run there will always be *volatility* in financial markets and particularly in stock markets. That is to say that they will move up and down a lot. In the long run, however, you have a high chance of making solid forward progress. The reason for this is that at a fundamental level when you invest in the stock market, you are actually investing in human progress, 'the most important investment theme in history', as we've already seen throughout the book.

[1] Macrobond data from MSCI World Equity Mid and MSCI Large Cap Total Return in GBP, 1 January 1972 - July 2022.

2 Invest regularly each month (automate)

Another key idea is to invest regularly every month, ideally automatically. This has three big benefits:

1. It overcomes the inertia we all naturally feel about doing admin. Getting an automatic payment set up once is relatively easy and then requires a minimum of effort going forwards. Once you've done it, you will not have to make complex decisions about when to put your money to work. This will maximize your chances of actually doing something with your finances sooner rather than later.
2. Investing regularly each month achieves something known as 'smoothing', 'averaging in' or 'dollar cost averaging'. To explain: the price of any financial asset or market goes up and down over time as we've seen. By investing each month, you improve your chances of buying in at a good *average* price and you ensure that you do not put a large amount of money into something just ahead of a crash.

   If anything you own does crash, by 'averaging in' each month you will automatically be investing when it is cheap in the months that follow that crash. Over time this will increase your chance of achieving market returns or at least close to market returns, rather than the lower-than-market returns that many investors make.
3. Investing automatically removes *you* from the equation. This is likely to be a very good idea as it minimizes the chance that you buy high and sell low because of how imperfect human psychology is, as we looked at above.

As we have already seen, the S&P 500 index in the US fell from about 1,500 in October 2007 to 666 in March 2009 (a 56% collapse). It then went from 666 all the way to around 6,000 at the time of writing. That's roughly 800% up since the bottom.

The problem is that human nature is such that if you had tried to time your investments to take advantage of these moves, you would almost certainly have got it wrong. In fact, the situation is actually worse than that. There is a high probability you would have sold low and bought high and timed your investments about as badly as it is possible to.

This is because we are hard-wired psychologically to get this sort of thing wrong. We humans are essentially herd animals. We pay a disproportionate amount of attention to what everyone else around us is doing. Much as we might fight it, very few of us have the knowledge or self-confidence to be truly contrarian.

When the market bottomed out at 666 in March 2009, nearly everyone on the news was going on about how risky stock market investment is and how much money everyone had just lost. As a result, you would have been highly unlikely to have considered putting money into the stock market.

Even more annoying, however: as the market recovered – 10% up, then 20%, 30%, 40%, all the way up to more than 800% – it would have been perfectly natural for you to say to yourself: 'Oh well. I've probably missed out now. The market is at an all-time high. I'm too late'. You will then not have invested.

After a few years of this, the next thought you might have would probably be something like: 'I really must sort this investment thing out. Look! The market is up more than 800%. It just keeps going up. Some of my friends have made a fortune. I've been avoiding it the whole time and missing out. Right. That's it. I'm in'.

You know the rest. Just as you decide it is time to put your money in the stock market again, along comes the next crash. You get absolutely flattened and spend the next decade licking your wounds. The cycle repeats. This happens to far too many investors time and time again. It is human nature. The other tragedy is that often when this happens, people give up on stock market investment altogether, preferring to stick to cash and property perhaps. This is highly likely to have a negative impact on your chances of optimizing your finances over a lifetime.

As we have already seen, the US stock market has returned an average of more than 10% a year in the century from January 1923 up to the time of writing. Most investors achieve many percentage points lower than this for all the reasons we've already covered. Given the power of compounding at higher rates of return, this has a huge negative impact on people's ability to become wealthy.

The antidote to all of this is to take yourself out of the equation by investing automatically each month and doing so for the very long run. Do not try to second guess what is going to happen. Do not try to time the market. Don't tell yourself 'I should buy this now or sell that now'. Do not ask supposed 'experts' what they think either. Just invest what you can afford, every month, without fail, into something sensible - (more on this shortly) until such time as you want to live on the proceeds (a time that will arrive sooner than most people believe is possible if you do this).

Let's come back to our example of the S&P 500. If you had been automating your payments monthly, you *would* have bought in at around 1,500 just before the crash (ouch), but then you also would have bought in every month after the crash, at 680, 750, 850, 930, 1,000 and so on – all the way up to around 6,000 today.

The net result of this approach is that you grind out consistent and meaningful returns (likely far higher than interest rates) through the economic cycle, no matter what is happening. Thanks to Einstein's 'eighth wonder of the world' – compound interest – the tortoise thrashes the hare and you end up with more money than most people think is possible.

3 Ignore the news and stick to your guns!

Another related point is the merit of completely ignoring the news when it comes to investment. We have already seen the importance of the big picture and the long game – of owning human progress – when it comes to investment success. The 'news' is essentially irrelevant to that big picture and long game. In fact, it is even worse than that. The more you pay attention to the financial news, the more likely you are to fall foul of human psychology – and buy high, sell low and reduce your investment returns.

People very often get in touch with me to say something like:

> Thanks so much for your book. Having read it, my wife and I really want to start investing but we are worried that now is probably a bad time because of coronavirus (or Brexit or Iran or fires in Los Angeles or a possible stock market crash). When do you think we should start investing please?

The answer to questions like this one is always the same. Stop thinking about the news and stop thinking about any kind of 'right time' to invest. The right time for you to start investing, if you haven't already started, is almost certainly right now.

There are always huge, scary stories in the news. If you were to go back through every single year since journalism was invented, you'd realize that there are 'big stories' week after week, month after month, year after year. This is how the media makes money, as we saw earlier in the book when we looked at the idea of negative press bias.

As serial entrepreneur Elon Musk has put it:

> The news tries to answer the question: what's the worst thing that happened on Earth today?

This gives everyone a heavily distorted view of the state of the world and, by extension, of financial markets. As I put it in one of my articles:

> People who have taken no time to study it or really understand it, think that the stock market is horribly risky. This is perhaps unsurprising given that the media goes bananas every time there is a 'massive crash' and that is most people's 'reality' when it comes to investment. The vast majority of the time that a sensible, diversified portfolio will gradually and entirely effectively build your wealth doesn't make front page news.

I have also written before about how human beings are hard-wired psychologically to focus on the extraordinary to the exclusion of the unremarkable, and how this reality is particularly relevant to investment. When financial markets crash, you will see lots of headlines like '£120 billion wiped off shares in a day'.

What you will never see is a headline that says:

THE GLOBAL ECONOMY HAS GROWN 670% SINCE 1985.

The gradual and significant increase in wealth that comes from investing over many years and sticking to your guns never makes the front pages of our newspapers. No television presenter ever says:

GREAT NEWS – THE STOCK MARKET HAS INCREASED BY 3% THIS MONTH.

As a result, most people have a horribly distorted view of financial markets. This is incredibly damaging to their chances of becoming wealthy. The most effective solution to this reality is to understand it, believe in human progress, automate your investments over long periods of time and completely ignore the news.

Taking this approach will very likely increase your investment returns, quite possibly by several percentage points – which can have a life-changing impact on your ability to become wealthy.

Perhaps more important still, it will reduce the administrative burden of your financial affairs and likely bring you real peace of mind. Regular, automated investment removes a great deal of stress and hassle and, arguably, also even helps you sleep at night. And it very likely increases the chance that you get your finances sorted. This is actually one of the most important considerations when it comes to investment given how many people never do! You have to be 'in it to win it', after all.

The lesson of history is that sticking to your guns over long periods of time will increase your chances of success. As Warren Buffett has put it:

> Lethargy bordering on sloth remains the cornerstone of our investment style.

Or, as his right-hand man, Charlie Munger, famously joked:

> Don't just do something, stand there!

Anyone invested in this reality who has also had the self-discipline to ignore the news along the way will also very likely enjoy wonderful peace of mind. Following the news is one of the main reasons most people do so badly with investment. It is also demonstrably bad for our mental health.

There is a great deal of academic and real-world evidence that you should totally and utterly ignore the news when thinking about investment. Whatever may or may not be happening in the world at the moment, the evidence of history is very consistently that you really don't need to worry in the slightest about 99.9% of the news stories of the day.

To live a good and prosperous life, with far less stress than most people seem to be suffering from these days, you need only arrange your financial affairs in a vaguely sensible way to benefit from humanity's inevitable progress and then leave well alone.

You must have confidence in your game plan and stick to your guns. Of course, doing this is far easier once you understand a bit about finance – given how much more confident you will be about what you are doing.

What is really important to stress again here is the importance of doing this over long periods of time. To maximize your chances of success you really do need to invest consistently over many years. When it comes to investing, patience gives you a huge advantage. Another reason so many people fail at this is because they just aren't patient enough and don't give the whole process enough time to work. This is why it is so important to set up something automatic alongside everything else you do in your life and just let it run its course.

All too often people who have only been investing for two or three years or, in some cases, even for only a few months or even weeks, can be disappointed that they haven't seen more progress, or even that they currently have less than they started with. Often people in this situation are considering giving up on investment.

This is one of the most important things to fight. The bad news is that building wealth invariably takes a long time, but the good news is that if you are willing to be patient and really commit to the process, the results can often be far beyond what most people think is possible.

It is important to stress that stock market returns are not smooth or consistent. A great deal of growth might come every few years over relatively short periods of time. Because of this, you want to ensure you have as much capital as you can invested at all times to ensure you capture that upside when it comes.

This reality is captured in a very well-known phrase in investing circles: 'Time in the market not timing the market.'

Wall Street vs Main Street

There is another important point to highlight here, which is just how often financial market performance is entirely unrelated to the news or even what is happening in the real economy.

The US stock market increased by 18.4% in 2020 and 28.7% in 2021. As the COVID-19 crisis was raging around us and lockdowns were wreaking havoc with economies – and people's lives – all over the world, the US stock market had two exceptionally big positive years!

If you had asked the average person with no knowledge of investment whether that would have been a good time to invest in the stock market, most people's answer would have been a resounding 'no'.

Too many people think that if there is a recession, there will be a stock market crash. This is yet another reason people avoid investing. This is a very simplistic view which, the evidence of history shows us, is often entirely wrong. There are plenty of professional investors, talking heads and financial advisers who get this wrong too.

Far more important than trying to work out what may or may not happen, based on the news or how you think the real economy is doing, successful investment is about doing something every month, from the moment you can afford to, for the rest of your life, and making sure that you are holding the right *mix* of assets over time.

If you do this, you should be in really good shape and have a really good chance of becoming wealthy over time. This is why I think this is the first thing you should focus on when it comes to your money and finances. Regular, automated payments into sensible investments such as your pension and other investment accounts, totalling 10% or more of your monthly income, every month, forever, should be a much higher priority than any kind of trading or putting money into things like crypto.

If you want to trade or invest in crypto then by all means look into that, but only after you've sorted out this more fundamental stuff.

Here, I am repeating the point made earlier when we looked at *investing vs trading*. So now let's look at how you might go about doing the admin and 'choosing something sensible...'

4 Use the idea of '100 minus your age'

One of the key things you are going to want to get right when you arrange your financial affairs is the trade-off between risk and reward. As we have seen, a key feature of investing in financial markets is that assets that might provide you with a higher percentage return tend to be riskier and have the potential to lose you lots of money in a crash (assuming you panic and sell, of course).

At the other end of the investment spectrum, things that are inherently safer will tend to give you lower investment returns. This has been particularly problematic in recent years, with returns on 'defensive' asset classes like cash and bonds at historically low, even negative levels in real terms (after inflation).

We've already covered a number of ways you might deal with this in the *accumulation* phase of your investment journey: by investing for the very long run, automating your investments every month and ignoring the news.

Another way to deal with the trade-off between higher-return, higher-risk assets and lower-return, lower-risk assets is to do your best to get the right *blend* of them over time.

One of the best-known ways of figuring out how to get this blend roughly right is something called '100 minus your age'. It's an idea that's often credited to John Bogle, the founder of the enormous investment group Vanguard.

For some decades now, many financial advisers and smart investors have used a basic rule of thumb that says that the percentage you invest in 'risky' or 'aggressive' assets like equities should be '100 minus your age', with the rest being held in 'lower-risk' or 'defensive' assets like cash, bonds or gold.

In the accumulation phase, these percentages give you an idea of how much you might invest each month into those respective asset classes. In the decumulation phase (when you're no longer investing each month but seeking to live on your money), they can give you a rough idea of how your pot should be allocated overall.

For example, if you are 25, you might invest roughly 75% of what you can afford each month into higher-return investments such as shares, and around 25% in more 'defensive' assets. Someone who is 75, might have only 25% of their money in riskier, higher-return assets, and 75% in lower-risk assets.

If you take this approach, you probably only need to review your investing plan every five years or so. Maybe do it on every 'round number' birthday: 30, 35, 40, 45, and so on. A 40-year-old might allocate 60% of what they can afford to invest each month to higher-risk assets and 40% to lower-risk assets. They'd let this run for five years, and then, at 45, they would tweak their portfolio so that it's 55% higher-risk assets and 45% lower-risk assets, and so on.

Traditionally, this approach used equites (shares) for the 'riskier' investments and bonds for 'less risky' ones.

'100 minus your age' is a very helpful idea when it comes to reducing your risk of loss as you get older, and closer to the point where you want to be able to live on your money. This will help you avoid that awful nightmare scenario of seeing your investment pot smashed to smithereens when you most need it – something that has happened to far too many people over the years – and entirely unnecessarily if you use this approach.

Like any idea in investment, '100 minus your age' isn't perfect. It was first devised in an era when bond returns were far higher than they are now.

The graph below shows the ten-year US Treasury interest rate going back to the 1960s. This is the interest rate used to decide

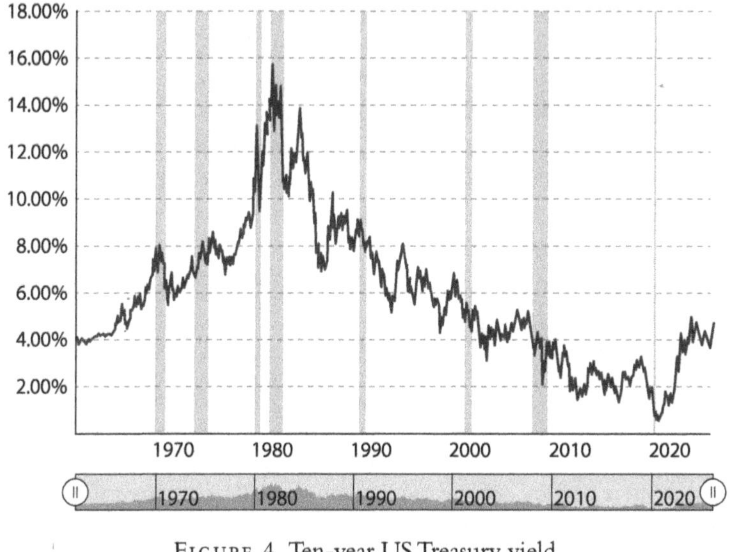

FIGURE 4 Ten-year US Treasury yield
(*source*: https://www.macrotrends.net/2016/10-year-treasury-bond-rate-yield-chart)

mortgage rates across the US. The treasuries market is the most liquid and widely traded bond market in the world, so this graph gives us a rough idea of the return an investor might expect on the 'defensive' bonds bit of their portfolio.

As you can see, interest rates were very low from the financial crisis of 2007 until quite recently. Even today, real interest rates after inflation are still historically low. For the last 50 years, however, bond rates have normally been between 4% and 8% and even as high as just under 16% in the early 1980s.

You can see from the graph that the average interest rate has been around 6%. It should be intuitively clear that '100 minus your age', using bonds for your 'defensive' allocation, will give you very different outcomes with bond rates at 1% or 2% to what you can achieve when they're more like 6% (if 50% of your portfolio is earning 6% versus earning 1–2%, for example).

For a fair chunk of the last 50 years, a retired person who had managed to build a nice big pot of money could expect to earn around 6% or even 8% a year just sitting with 100% of their money in bonds. For anyone lucky enough to have, say, $1 million invested, that was around $60,000-80,000 a year of 'risk-free' income.

With real interest rates now much lower – this number has fallen a long way. It is much harder to earn enough of a real return on your money, particularly when you factor in real inflation.

This reality has had serious consequences, as you might imagine, particularly for people at or near retirement. Low interest (bond) rates have been one of the most important considerations for investors for the last few years. As a result, '100 minus your age' is perhaps a good deal less useful an idea today than it was when real interest (bond) rates were far higher.

Life expectancy and retirement age

The other consideration here is life expectancy. Amazingly enough, this has increased by around 30 years in the last century in the developed world. Scientists predict that this trend will continue. Many children born today have a good chance of living well past 100. If we are living 30 or even 40 years longer today than when '100 minus your age' was conceived, then presumably we need to take that into account?

A similar and related point concerns *retirement age*. If people used to retire at 60 and now many knowledge workers might continue to work until 70 or beyond, then there's a whole decade or more during which their money might be better off earning a higher return, given that it's not yet needed to generate income to live on.

'120 minus your age?'

Given what has happened to real interest rates, life expectancy and retirement age, some financial advisers advocate simply changing the rule to '110 – or even 120 – minus your age'.

If real interest rates are low and we are living and working longer, then perhaps we can afford to keep more of our money in 'riskier', higher-return investments for longer in the hope of building a bigger retirement pot.

People just haven't been saving and investing enough

A related (and more negative) point concerns the fact that in the last two or three decades the vast majority of people in the developed world have not been saving or investing enough.

For most of the 1950s right up until the 1980s, Americans saved around 9% of their income, on average. This had fallen to about 2% by the time of the financial crisis in 2007.

The same has been true in most of the rest of the developed world – certainly in the 'Anglo-Saxon' bits of it. As interest rates have fallen and credit has become far easier to get hold of, a depressingly large percentage of the population have chosen to save less and borrow more. This is the absolute 180-degree opposite of what they 'should' have done. It's actually one of the key reasons for the financial crises of recent decades too.

It is perhaps worth contrasting our behaviour in the Anglo-American world with savings habits in many parts of Asia. In China, for example, savings rates have traditionally been north of 30% of income! In Singapore, citizens must invest 20% of their monthly income into the government pension fund (the Central Provident Fund), and employers then add another 17%. That is 37% of what you earn being invested in your future (and Singapore's future, too).

It is also perhaps worth contrasting the growth experience of such countries in recent decades as a result. Singapore has grown at more than 6% a year on average since the 1970s – a far higher rate than the US or UK. Consider also that GDP per capita (average annual income) in Singapore in 2023 was very high, at just below $85,000.

Of course, high savings rates aren't the only reason for high rates of economic growth in these countries. They don't entirely explain why Singaporeans are so wealthy, but they've certainly played a significant role.

This has been positive for US shares

This has also been one of the key drivers of the exceptional performance of the S&P 500 in recent years – as counter-intuitive as that might sound. This is because millions of baby boomers – who are now at or near retirement – need to keep a higher proportion of their wealth in the stock market rather than in bonds.

Millions of Americans, and the financial advisers who serve them, have been forced to chase higher returns by investing more in the stock market. This, combined with the rise of inexpensive ETF products, has created an incredibly powerful upward spiral in the world's largest and most liquid stock markets – and the S&P 500 as the 'Big Daddy' of them all.

In many ways, this is what has been driving the huge increase in value of big tech companies in recent years. Whether the result of all of this is a bubble or not and what has come up must (eventually) come down, remains to be seen. It's certainly something to be careful about.

Happily, the idea of '100 minus your age' can help you do just that, as does investing every month over many years and ignoring the news, as we've already discussed.

'100 minus your age' vs the '60/40 portfolio'

Before we go on to look in more detail at how you might implement a '100 minus your age' approach for your investments, it's worth looking at a couple of other broad approaches to investing: something called the '60/40 portfolio' and what you might describe as the 'market purist' approach of investing *only* in shares.

'100 minus your age' is an arguably more advanced version of the '60/40 portfolio', which has been around since the 1950s. '60/40' refers to a portfolio holding 60% in shares and 40% in bonds. Rather than have to bother to change your allocation every five to ten years based on '100 minus your age', the idea was that you could just keep a 60/40 allocation for your entire investing life.

The idea came primarily from Harry Markowitz and William Sharpe, both of whom received the Nobel Prize in Economics for their work on 'Modern Portfolio Theory'.

The 60/40 mix was a solid 'set and forget' approach to investment for roughly six decades from the 1960s onwards. A 60% exposure to the stock market provided good returns and the 40% in bonds protected the downside and reduced losses overall when the stock market crashed. From 1961 to 2021 this approach averaged about 9.3% annual returns but with lower volatility and risk of loss than just investing in the stock market – a great outcome for those who used the strategy.

The reason 60/40 worked so well for much of that time was that bonds and shares were what is called 'negatively correlated'. When shares fell, bonds went up. This meant that the bond component of the 60/40 portfolio could protect an investor during stock market crashes.

In recent years, however, bonds and shares have become 'positively correlated', which means that the strategy has stopped working and there are concerns that it may not be as successful in future.

Usually if the stock market crashes, there is a 'flight to quality', which means that worried investors sell 'aggressive' shares to buy 'defensive' bonds. This bids up the price of bonds and is why the two assets can often be negatively correlated.

This stops working, however, when investors expect interest rates to rise. Bond prices fall when interest rates rise. With the higher inflation that we've seen in recent years, investors have expected higher interest rates, which has caused many bond prices to fall, often by a lot.

This is why many market watchers fear that the 60/40 portfolio is unlikely to work as well in future as it has in the past. You may, therefore, be better served by the more nuanced idea of '100 minus your age', and by using a variety of 'aggressive' and 'defensive' investments, not just shares and bonds.

100% shares – the 'market purist' approach

Another approach we should at least mention in passing is the idea that all you need to do is buy shares. There are many sensible financial market commentators who have suggested that you may only need to own 'the market' (by which they usually mean the US market – essentially the S&P 500). That is to say that you don't need to think about 'aggressive' versus 'defensive' at all. You can just buy 'aggressive' shares throughout your investing life.

One famous advocate of this approach is Warren Buffett. Buffett, and others like him, are on record suggesting that all someone need do when it comes to investment is simply buy the market each month, every month for many years. This stance is particularly popular at the moment given how long and strong the run in the S&P 500 has been.

A key point to make about this stance is that it works well if you are very wealthy. As we saw previously, a 50% market correction for a 65-year-old with $1 million will be far worse than it will be for a 30-year-old with $10,000 and a lifetime of investment ahead of them. For the 65-year-old that sort of 'draw-down' could be catastrophic or, at the very least, very stressful to live through.

But what about someone worth $10 million? After a 50% market correction, they would still have $5 million in their investment accounts even if they were 100% allocated to the stock market. As should be more or less obvious, this would be much less catastrophic than a 50% correction for someone with 'only' $1 million!

Very wealthy people can take the risk of being almost entirely exposed to the stock market because they will still more than likely have enough to live on if the market crashes. They can 'ride out' the volatility until the market goes back up again without it having much of an impact on their lives. This is why very wealthy folks like Warren Buffett tend to be such 'market purists'.

If you are a very high earner, start investing early enough and make strong returns, you have a good chance of ending up with several million dollars or pounds.

If you manage to achieve this, you can then afford to continue to take more risk with your portfolio, because a big stock market correction is unlikely to affect you in terms of your ability to cover the key costs of living your life. This is clearly a wonderful position to be in.

I would argue that most people, however, will still want to ensure they have the right mix of 'aggressive' and 'defensive' investments over time, given that a big stock market crash will likely be far more problematic for them. Hopefully this makes sense.

What to do?

So, we have just covered the challenges associated with the traditional '60/40 portfolio'. We've also looked at the fact that a 'market purist' approach of owning only shares will expose you to a good deal of volatility and is, therefore, probably only a good idea if you're very wealthy – and pretty psychologically strong too.

Some kind of '100 minus your age' approach may be a kind of "goldilocks" option then – one that may suit the majority of people. What this means in plain English, is that you will split whatever you can afford to invest each month into 'aggressive' vs 'defensive' investments based roughly on your age (after you've paid down expensive debt and saved up your 'rainy day' pot of course).

You then have two broad decisions to make:

1 Whether to use 100, 110 or 120 to calculate how to split your investments.
2 *Which* 'aggressive' and 'defensive' investments to make.

Let's look at each of these in turn...

Which number to use

Deciding whether to use 100, 110 or 120 minus your age to calculate your split will depend on your own personal circumstances. Here are some things to think about:

1 How comfortable with risk versus how risk-averse you are overall. If you are inherently conservative, then you might use 100 to make your calculation. If you have the mental

strength to endure periods where your investments could be down quite a lot, then you might use 120 as the basis for your calculation. Be warned however, that relatively few people have this mental strength.

2 How much you earn; this tends to be related to the last point. Although this is by no means always the case, people who earn more or who have significant wealth already tend to be more comfortable with risk – because they can afford to be. The more surplus you have, over and above what you need to fund life's essentials, the more ambitious you can afford to be with your investments. If you are a high earner, you might be more inclined to use the 120 number as opposed to the 100 number. That having been said, this will be a matter of personal choice. There are plenty of wealthy people who are inherently conservative when it comes to their wealth. Many of them will tell you that this is why they became wealthy!

3 How old you want to be when you retire. Some people make enough to 'retire' in their thirties, and others are so passionate about what they do that they're still loving their work (and hopefully making good money doing it) in their late seventies and beyond. The longer you are employed and earning a decent income, the longer it will be before you need to rely on your investments to sustain you. This means, all other things being equal, that you can afford to invest in more 'aggressive' assets for longer and might, therefore, use 120 rather than 100 in your calculations here. That having been said, if you use the 120 number, bear in mind that you could still have 50% of your money in higher-risk assets at the age of 70. That is, perhaps, quite a bold call – unless you're fairly wealthy and comfortable with risk.

There is no 'one-size-fits-all' 'right' answer here, but the whole concept of '100 minus your age' can give you a solid big-picture idea of how you might set up roughly the right balance of investments to increase your chances of making solid investment returns over time and minimize the risk of a large loss.

Whichever number you choose to use, below I have provided a simple 'ready-reckoner' table to help you work out how you might think about allocating your investments based on your age and attitude to risk:

TABLE 2 'Ready-reckoner' table

Your age	100 minus rule		110 minus rule		120 minus rule	
	Aggres.	Defen.	Aggres.	Defen.	Aggres.	Defen.
	%	%	%	%	%	%
100	0	100	10	90	20	80
95	5	95	15	85	25	75
90	10	90	20	80	30	70
85	15	85	25	75	35	65
80	20	80	30	70	40	60
75	25	75	35	65	45	55
70	30	70	40	60	50	50
65	35	65	45	55	55	45
60	40	60	50	50	60	40
55	45	55	55	45	65	35
50	50	50	60	40	70	30
45	55	45	65	35	75	25
40	60	40	70	30	80	20
35	65	35	75	25	85	15
30	70	30	80	20	90	10
25	75	25	85	15	95	5
20	80	20	90	10	100	0
15	85	15	95	5	100	0
10	90	10	100	0	100	0
5	95	5	100	0	100	0
0	100	0	100	0	100	0

Five-year reviews

If you take this approach, you will probably only need to review your investing plan relatively infrequently.

Every five years or so, you might sit down and spend an hour or three ensuring that your financial arrangements are sensible and, preferably, on autopilot. Then you can forget about it for another five years.

This whole approach can give you real peace of mind and makes things a great deal less cumbersome than the approach so many people take, chopping and changing all the time.

Five years is also a period of time that will give your investments the best chance to make you a positive return. Another rookie mistake people make all too often is to invest in something that then has a negative few months (or even a few days or weeks!), and then sell out and move into something else that is doing 'better'.

This goes back to the point we made earlier about human psychology, where we said that financial products are one of the few things that people tend to buy when they're expensive and sell when they're cheap. Giving up on an investment fund after a few months or even, frankly, after a few years and switching to a fund that has been doing 'better' is one of the many reasons most investors return less than the market does.

As we have seen, sticking to your guns for long periods of time is really important – particularly if you're buying every month and dollar cost averaging anyway – which means that you will be buying any of your investments that are down more cheaply each month whilst they are down.

As Bloomberg journalist John Stepek put it rather brilliantly in one of his articles:

> There are many roads to ruin in the markets – some of them longer than others – but one sure-fire way is to set out as a buy-and-hold investor and then attempt to turn into a market timer during a bout of market panic. This will do more damage to your portfolio than following one approach or the other.[2]

---

2 John Stepek, 'Is this another buying opportunity? Or is it the start of something bigger?', *MoneyWeek*, 11 October 2018. https://moneyweek.com/496454/market-crash-buying-opportunity-or-the-start-of-something-bigger. Last accessed 1 August 2025.

It's crucial to stay focused on the long run and stick to your guns. Some version of '100 minus your age' applied to how you invest can help you work out whether you are broadly in the right mix of things and on the right track. This approach will make you far less likely to make the mistakes that so many people make that are born of panic and silly headlines from a global press that focuses 99.99% of its attention on the bad things that only happen 0.01% of the time.

Now that we've covered these four key approaches to investing, in the next chapter we'll go on to look at how you might bring all these ideas together and get things sorted!

12
Bringing it all together

So far in this section of the book we've looked at:

- the crucial difference between investing and trading
- the two key investing phases in your life: accumulation, when you build wealth over many years, and decumulation, when you are able to live on the wealth you have built
- the role played by human psychology and the painful mathematics of the 'break-even fallacy'.

We've also looked at four ideas that can help you 'invest so that crashes don't matter':

- Investing for the long run, ideally the very long run
- Investing regularly each month, ideally automatically
- Doing your best to ignore the news and stick to your plan
- Using some version of '100 minus your age' to get your mix of 'aggressive' and 'defensive' assets roughly right.

I also made the point that there is far less of a relationship between 'Wall Street' and 'Main Street' than most people, including plenty of investment professionals, realize. It is entirely possible for the economy to be doing pretty badly and for there to be lots of horrible stories in the news but for financial markets to do pretty well.

To illustrate this, we looked at the example of how strong the performance of American shares was during the COVID-19 crisis.

Which 'aggressive' and 'defensive' investments?

Having come this far, I hope that you now have a rough idea of the sort of approach you would like to take with your investments. Hopefully you have worked out how much you can afford to invest each month and roughly how to allocate that money between 'aggressive' and 'defensive' assets.

The final piece of the jigsaw puzzle concerns which specific investments you might consider.

A key first point to make here is the value of *keeping things simple*, particularly as you start out. There are obviously many, many thousands of things out there that you could invest in. Given how many options there are, there is a serious risk of 'paralysis by analysis'.

One of the biggest enemies of investment success is *inertia*, and the fact that this prevents lots of people from doing anything at all. Having far too many things to choose from often causes people to give up and do nothing – with disastrous results for their ability to become wealthy over time. Many millions of people have fallen foul of this.

Another mistake people make is to massively over-complicate matters. All too often, inexperienced investors will have no simple regular savings and investing plan, but will instead be spending huge amounts of time trying to learn incredibly complicated trading strategies, or looking at crypto and other very high-risk things.

This has a low probability of success. A much better approach is to choose a handful of simple investments and put your money to work every month on autopilot, forever.

When it comes to 'aggressive' investments, arguably the very simplest thing you might do is to own a large equity market of some kind. You will hopefully recall that the original idea of '100 minus your age' was to put *x*% in 'aggressive' equities (shares) and the rest in 'defensive' bonds based on your age.

Part of the reason for this rather simplistic approach had to do with the financial products that existed when this idea was first formulated. Go back a few decades and financial services weren't very sophisticated – at least as compared to today.

There weren't that many financial products available for the ordinary investor back then. If you were a normal investor based in the US, your financial adviser was just about able to get you positioned in the Dow Jones and US Treasuries (bonds). If you were based in the UK, you would probably have been steered toward the FTSE 30 (as it was before 1984) and UK gilts (UK government bonds).

Today, things are completely different and very much better! Nowadays it is possible to invest in pretty much anything that you can think of using Exchange Traded Funds as we saw earlier in the book (in Chapter 8) when we covered shares and funds.

You will hopefully recall that we looked at the idea of investing in American shares, using the S&P 500, or investing in a broader global index like the MSCI World, MSCI All-Country World or FTSE All-World, all of which include companies from all over the world.

Using one of these for the 'aggressive' proportion of any money you want to save and invest each month is a very simple approach. If you do this regularly over many years, the evidence of history is that it could deliver a great result. Of course, you must ensure you've paid off any debt and saved up a 'rainy day' pot of cash first.

Don't forget what 'aggressive' means

You need to remember why these sorts of investments should only sit on the 'aggressive' side of your portfolio. In 2008, the MSCI All-Country World Index and the S&P 500 both fell around 40%. They also crashed early in 2020 at the beginning of the COVID-19 crisis, before bouncing strongly through the rest of the year – which was great for people who were buying monthly, of course.

It is very important to remember that, while these sorts of investments could give you roughly 10% returns on average *over long periods of time*, and even 20–30% years now and then, they can and will have big down years from time to time.

This needn't be a problem for your ability to grow wealth over the long term *if* you are properly and appropriately diversified (by using something like '100 minus your age'), if you are buying regularly every month over many years, and if you have a plan, stick to your guns and ignore the news – but you *must* have just such a plan and you must stick to it. If you do all of these things, you have a solid chance of building wealth.

When it comes to how you might get the 'aggressive' proportion of your investment capital to work, one of these large index funds should do a perfectly good job for most people. Each of them will give you exposure to hundreds or even thousands of companies and to global growth and human progress more generally. They are large and liquid, cheap to buy and can be purchased in investment accounts all over the world.

Choosing an ETF that tracks one or another of these indices keeps things nice and simple, which will likely increase the probability that you will actually get started.

Of course, there are lots of other things you could invest in, but simply having exposure to a big equity index is a good example of the 'Pareto Principle', which says you can get most of the result you need without complicating things too much. Over time, if you become particularly interested in finance and investment, you might consider any number of other kinds of 'aggressive' investments, but it is probably worth keeping things simple for several years before you do that.

Investing in a big equity index every month for many years will very likely get you 80% or even more of the result you want in terms of building wealth.

If you buy a big equity index each month, you don't have to spend hours puzzling over complicated considerations about what to do with your money and you will very likely get a perfectly solid result over time. As we have seen, this is the view of a lot of very smart, wealthy and successful investors, including folks like Warren Buffett. Plenty of successful entrepreneurs, captains of industry, and smarter-than-average celebrities use this approach as well.

What about 'defensive' investments?

As we have just seen, choosing a fund to get the 'aggressive' bit of your investment capital to work is relatively simple. You need only own a big stock market index to cover that pretty well and get most of the result you're looking for.

The 'defensive' bit is quite a bit harder nowadays. This is because real interest rates (after inflation) have been so low or even negative for a long time.

As we saw earlier, traditionally the 'defensive' bit of a '100 minus your age' approach would have been allocated to bonds. For quite a few years now, following that strategy has been problematic. With interest rates and, by extension, bond returns being as low as they have been since the financial crisis of 2007–8, returns on many 'defensive' investments have been very low historically.

As interest rates have risen in recent years, this has also caused the price of many bonds to fall a long way, because bond prices fall when interest rates rise. This is the reason the '60/40 portfolio' stopped working a few years ago.

Luckily for most readers of this book, this is a great deal less problematic for you than it is for people who are older. If you are under the age of 30, you don't need to have very much of your money in 'defensive' investments. You might even consider having none at all, given that you are so many years away from retirement.

There is also a chance that interest rates in the years ahead will be higher than they have been in recent years. What this means is that by the time you might want to invest a big chunk of your money in more 'defensive' asset classes, you could be facing a better environment than people have had to contend with for the last couple of decades, with higher potential returns on your 'defensive' investments.

In the meantime, however, there is one asset that you might consider as a 'defensive' place to invest, even now: gold.

Gold can reasonably be considered to be a 'defensive' asset. Since the 1990s, it has been less volatile than shares and slightly more volatile than bonds. It is also conventionally considered to be what is called an 'inflation hedge'. This means that it is potentially a good thing to own if real inflation is high.

Owning inflation

'Gold is money. Everything else is just credit.'

– John Pierpoint (JP) Morgan

You will hopefully remember that stuff goes up in price when there is inflation. In fact, inflation *is* an increase of the price of stuff, if you think about it; these are two sides of the same coin. When it comes to investing, you might think about 'stuff' as basically being 'commodities'. If we want to own inflation, we might think about owning some commodities. We looked at these ideas earlier in the book.

If you own a big equity index you will already have a certain amount of natural exposure to commodities (and global currencies for that matter) because several of the companies in that index will be involved with commodities in some shape or form, or will own them.

One relatively simple way to have a little bit more direct exposure is to own gold. Gold is a commodity, but it is also something of a special case. Not only is it a commodity, but it has also been used as money for much of history; it is a 'monetary metal'.

As we've already seen earlier in this book, money is actually just a technology. In many ways it is also one of the most valuable technologies we have ever invented as a species. This is why anything that can be used as money tends to be pretty valuable.

What is interesting about gold is that it has several inherent qualities that have made it particularly suitable to playing the role of money. Out of all the raw materials available on our planet, gold became very widely accepted as money because it was uniquely able to do the job.

Gold is durable, divisible, malleable, portable, recognizable, and almost optimally scarce. Some of the other things we looked at in the introduction to the book that were once used as money – stones, tea, feathers, timber, seashells – weren't great raw materials for money because they didn't have all of these qualities, and weren't sufficiently scarce either. On the other hand, very special, rare things like diamonds and other precious stones were too scarce.

This is why human beings chose gold as money, time after time over thousands of years, in places that were thousands of miles away from each other, and gold continues to be worth many trillion dollars at the time of writing.

So, if you want to get some exposure to commodities, owning some gold is an easy way to do that – especially because it is very easy to invest in gold in many places in the world.

Many commodities are very volatile and a risky investment as a result. Take copper for example: copper is a metal, just like gold, but its use is basically 100% industrial. As a result, if the world is manufacturing fewer cars or building fewer skyscrapers, the copper price can fall a long way. Gold can have down years too, but tends to be much less volatile, partly because of its role in the monetary system.

Gold has been a solid 'defensive' asset for most of the 21st century, having delivered high-single-digit or even low-double-digit average annual returns in most major currencies in that time. This could well continue with so many countries in the world choosing to print money. Remember, if there is a relatively fixed supply of gold, but a great deal more money is being created, then the price of gold will increase over time in terms of that money. This has been happening for a long time and will likely continue to happen.

Even though gold has performed very well for more than two decades, it still only makes up about 1% of the total financial assets in the world.[1] As recently as the 1960s, this figure was more like 5%. If it heads back towards being a larger share of financial assets in the years ahead, this could continue to support the price for a long time to come. A Gold Council Survey in 2024 found that 69% of central banks in the world are planning to increase their gold reserves, which suggests that this could indeed be the direction of travel.

You can never predict exactly what financial markets are going to do, but gold could serve as a solid 'defensive' asset to complement your more 'aggressive' investments in something like a big stock market index.

How to buy gold

If you do decide you want to invest in some gold, there are three key ways you can do that, each of which has its pros and cons. These are:

1. Buying actual 'physical' gold, and hiding it in your home. Ideally this should involve a safe – or, perhaps a spade!
2. Buying physical gold using a company that specializes in such things, and having them store it for you.
3. Buying a precious metals Exchange Traded Fund (ETF) or Exchange Traded Commodity (ETC).

1 Buying physical and taking delivery

Wherever you are in the world, there should be various ways that you might be able to buy gold. It is important to use a reputable company

[1] https://www.gold.org/goldhub/research/market-primer/gold-market-primer-market-size-and-structure

to ensure that you are actually buying the real thing. It is vital not to cut corners here.

In London, there is a famous company called Sharps Pixley. They have been selling gold to British investors since 1778. They even have an actual shop in the historic St. James's neighbourhood, which is quite cool – and well worth a visit. Elsewhere in the world, you should be able to find a gold bullion dealer in most major cities.

Gold purists (or 'gold bugs' as they are known) will generally tell you that buying physical bullion in this way and actually taking delivery of it so you can look at it and touch it, is the only way to go when buying gold. As far as they are concerned, any other 'synthetic' kind of gold ownership is to be avoided.

The main reason they believe this is because there is much more 'theoretical' gold in the world – that is, financial instruments that seek to represent gold – than actual physical metal. This is clear if you look at estimates of how much gold has ever actually been mined compared to the total value of the gold market.

A generally accepted rough estimate is that there is anywhere between 50 and 100 times as much 'theoretical' or 'paper' gold as real. Gold bugs worry that this means that if there was ever a 'run' on gold, meaning that everyone who theoretically owned gold wanted to take possession of the gold they owned, as many as 99 out of 100 of those people wouldn't be able to get their hands on it! This is why gold bugs insist on being able to have their gold in their possession.

The counterargument to this rather alarmist position is that there can (and maybe even should) be significantly more 'paper' gold in the world. The same logic underpins banking. Banks only hold a fraction of what they lend out in the economy. Ultimately, the global financial system works on what are called 'fractional reserves'. There is vastly more credit out there than actual money in banks. If traders are making bets with each other, the existence of physical metal only becomes relevant for the tiny minority of contracts where physical delivery actually takes place. Most contracts are just a bet that something will move a certain way over some period of time, and the participants close out these bets with each other without going anywhere near actually owning the underlying asset.

This is a bit like something called the 'velocity of money' in the economy more generally. Say you pay $20 for a haircut; the hairdresser spends that $20 on a bottle of wine; the retailer, distributor and wine-grower spend that same $20 on three other things; and so on. One $20 bill has created hundreds of dollars' worth of activity in the economy and no one argues there was 'only one $20 bill' so that 'shouldn't work'.

That said, the system does leave itself open to manipulation, and it isn't difficult to demonstrate that even central banks don't trust each other when it comes to real, physical gold holdings these days. That being the case, you as a private individual might be even more nervous.

There are two problems with buying actual, physical gold, however: first of all, you will need quite a lot of money. At the time of writing, even just one gram of gold – the smallest amount of physical gold you can buy – will cost you as much as $100, and this number could well increase in future.

The other problem is that there is a security risk in doing so. Unless you have an expensive safe that is built into your property (one that can't be picked up and carried away by thieves), or you are willing to dig a pretty large hole in your garden somewhere and draw yourself an 'x marks the spot' treasure map, there is always a risk that physical bullion that you have might be stolen. It is for this reason that many people opt for the second of our methods:

2 Buying physical and paying a company to store it for you

For those who are a little less paranoid than the ultimate purist gold bugs, there are plenty of companies who will let you buy physical gold and store it with them for a fee.

One of these is a company called BullionVault. If you want to own gold and other precious metals such as silver, BullionVault is a web-based service that enables you to do so without taking delivery. At the time of writing, they are the world's largest company of this kind, with more than 100,000 clients who own more than $4 billion of precious metals between them.

The gold is held legally in your name and you can choose to keep it stored in places like Switzerland or Singapore, so that the US or British government won't be able to confiscate it if it ever comes to that. Remember, if this sounds like a crazy conspiracy theory to you, it has happened before – and in living memory. It was illegal for private citizens in the US to hold gold from 1933 to 1974. It is entirely possible that this kind of thing may happen again, in which case you will be glad that you are in physical possession of your bullion or, failing that, that you have it stored in Switzerland or Singapore, assuming such countries continue to permit private ownership.

Setting up an account with BullionVault is easy. You register just as you would with a site like Amazon or Facebook and you get an email immediately. You can then just transfer money from your bank account as you would with paying any bill or transferring money to a friend.

It should be noted that the minimum monthly charge for storing gold with BullionVault is $4, which might be quite a high percentage cost if you only have a relatively small amount to invest. This isn't really a big problem, however, because as you add more and more to your account over time these percentages will come down pretty quickly.

Buying gold is a bit like buying insurance. You buy your car insurance every month, because if you are unlucky enough to have an accident, you will get a payout. You buy gold regularly because if there is a monetary crisis or other serious market volatility you will be glad you own some. The thought process, therefore, is a little different to other investments.

As we've seen, there is a chance that the gold price could be structurally stronger in future as governments all over the world continue to print money. Gold can be a 'defensive' asset and an insurance policy of sorts. As a result, you might argue that you shouldn't worry overly about paying relatively small fees for commission and storage as you build your position over time.

3 Buying a precious metals ETC (Exchange Traded Commodity)

As we have seen, one of the problems with the precious metals market generally is that there is vastly more 'theoretical' gold in the world (i.e. trading as financial instruments that seek to represent gold) than there is actual gold and – for this reason – real gold 'purists' insist on taking physical delivery.

The trouble with this – taking physical delivery, that is – is that you are then faced with a choice between two potentially slightly annoying alternatives:

1 Take delivery of your highly valuable metal and worry about where to store it and how to secure it.
2 Pay someone else to store and secure it for you.

The first option comes with the inherent risk that someone might one day stumble upon your stash and steal it – or with the cost of having a half-decent safe installed in your home. The second obviously adds another layer of cost of ownership, although you might argue these costs are not that big a worry over time.

One way to get exposure to precious metals which neatly sidesteps these two problems – to a certain extent, at least – is to invest in them by using an ETC (Exchange Traded Commodity). These are similar to the ETFs we covered earlier in the book.

Physical vs swap-based ETCs

An ETC is simply a financial vehicle that trades like a share on the stock market and gives you exposure to any number of different underlying investments – in this case gold. There are two broad types of ETC: 'swap-based' and 'physical'. The first uses futures or options contracts to replicate the performance of the underlying asset (in this case, physical bullion). If that sounds rather complicated, all you need to know is that this is essentially a 'synthetic' way of replicating the underlying asset.

Unless you are a shorter-term trader and understand these things, you should almost certainly use *physically* backed ETCs (rather than synthetic or swap-based). A physically backed ETC will actually own essentially the same amount of physical bullion as there is invested in the fund.

When someone puts money into a physically backed ETC, the provider will add that amount of gold to their holdings (within a certain time period). Theoretically, you shouldn't then have a problem monetizing your gold ownership if there is some sort of huge global crisis. A physically backed ETC will always own the actual physical gold that you are entitled to and have enough 'value' in the fund to pay out. Still, though, many purists argue that even this isn't good enough.

First of all, *in extremis*, a government could pass legislation allowing it to confiscate gold 'in the system' like this. As we have already seen, this has happened before in many countries, including in 'free-market' America, so an ETC may not be as safe and reliable as having physical bullion hidden in the bottom of your cat's litter box.

Secondly, your ability to get your hands on your precious metals or benefit from owning an ETC will also rely, to a certain degree, on the ETC provider's continued existence. This touches on something called 'counterparty risk'. Basically, this means that if the company providing your ETC goes bust, you might not get your money or your gold back.

In the short- and medium-term, neither of these things is particularly likely to happen but if you have quite a lot invested in precious metals, especially as you get older, you should probably own physical gold in some shape or form and consider using ETCs as an option for any additional short- or medium-term exposure you'd like to have when you get a bit more expert at such things.

What about currency?

A final thing to highlight here is the fact that you can buy physical gold ETCs that are denominated in different currencies. Sometimes people wonder about whether they should buy an ETC in pounds or dollars, for example. I would argue that this doesn't actually matter that much.

Whatever currency the product is quoted in, it will reflect the relative value of gold in that currency and any small differences in cost, due to fluctuating exchange rates are not worth worrying about.

It is worth repeating that buying precious metals is a bit like buying insurance. You buy them because if there is a monetary crisis or other serious market volatility you could get a big payout. This is why you probably don't need to worry too much about relatively minor issues like which currency ETC you choose to own.

A note on silver

Before we move on, it is worth noting that silver is often thought of as an alternative to gold. It is also a precious metal, with a long track record of having been used as money. This having been said, silver tends to be far more volatile than gold. Silver tends to amplify whatever gold does in terms of price performance. If the price of gold goes up by 10%, silver might go up by two or more times that amount. This is also true when the price goes down, which makes it a fundamentally riskier asset.

The silver market is much smaller than the gold market, and a significant proportion of the demand for silver comes from industrial uses, which can fluctuate with economic conditions. Silver can be an interesting investment from time to time, but it is important to stress that it is probably best not to think about it as being 'defensive'.

A note on gold miners

The last thing to at least mention in passing when it comes to gold is that it is important to differentiate between owning gold and investing in *companies* involved in the gold market, like mining companies or funds that invest in gold mining.

Investing in gold mining companies is a far riskier investment than buying gold itself. Gold can reasonably be considered to be a 'defensive' investment. Gold miners are high-risk shares which can lose you a great deal of money if you get it wrong.

Some last few things!

We're now on the home straight as we head towards the end of the book. Before we sign off, there are a handful of other topics we need to at least touch on in passing.

Regular monthly investing vs getting a lump sum to work

Let's think for a moment about the difference between regular monthly investment of a certain part of your income and thinking about how to invest a lump sum you already have.

Regular monthly investment

For most people, as we've seen, regular investment is the foundation for building wealth. If you invest what you can afford every month without fail into something sensible and do that until such time as you want to live on the proceeds, there is a solid chance that you can get to a six- or even seven-figure sum over a lifetime of investing, almost no matter how little you begin with or how much you earn. You really can expect to become meaningfully wealthy over time.

As we saw earlier in our section about finding the money: 'There is a simple formula for becoming wealthy that is well understood by the rich and unchanged since humans invented money: live on less than you earn and invest the rest…'

I stressed that you are going to want to be saving and investing at least 10% of your monthly income, and we explored how you might make that happen. We have also looked at many of the reasons why investing regularly every month is such a good approach.

Investing regularly and automatically each month should remove a huge amount of stress and hassle and is a key factor in keeping things manageable and being successful in the long run.

A great book about this kind of investing is the classic *Rich Dad Poor Dad* by Robert Kiyosaki, where he describes this process as 'paying yourself first'.

Lump sums

That said, you may already have a *lump sum* that you would like to get to work. Perhaps you have already saved up tens or even hundreds of thousands of dollars or pounds, or you are lucky enough to have inherited a significant sum recently, or maybe you've sold a business or property.

If this describes you, then you will of course want to be very careful that you don't end up investing all of that money in something which then crashes not long afterwards. Too many people have made that mistake over the years and it can be very painful.

One relatively simple way to get around this concern is to divide up your lump sum and pay one-tenth or one-twelfth of it into your investments each month for the next ten to twelve months along with whatever else you intend to save and invest monthly.

This will achieve the 'averaging in' or 'smoothing' I described earlier in the book, ensuring that you don't fall foul of a crash shortly after putting a large amount of money into something.

This is a crucial approach when it comes to any 'aggressive' investments you might decide to make. It is obviously less of a worry if you're putting that money into anything 'defensive', which is less likely to experience a big crash.

Rebalancing

One other final consideration is something called 'rebalancing'. This is the idea that you need to return your investments to the right percentage allocation every now and then as they will move around as a result of your investment performance.

If you have decided to invest 80% in something 'aggressive' and 20% in something 'defensive,' after a few years you might find that your investment performance has moved you quite a long way away from that percentage allocation.

The solution to this is called 'rebalancing'. Once a year or so, you'd look at the assets you hold and sell the ones that have gone up most to buy the ones that have gone up least (or even fallen), to get back to your desired 80/20 allocation.

Five-year reviews

As a final reminder, if you are using the idea of '100 minus your age' you might also shift some of your overall allocation from 'aggressive' to 'defensive' assets every five years or so – as we looked at earlier in the book. You might find the ready-reckoner table in Chapter 11 useful for helping you get this roughly right over time.

In summary

In this section of the book we have:

- explained the crucial difference between investing and trading
- looked at four key investing ideas:
  - Investing for the long run, and ideally the *very* long run
  - Investing regularly each month and automating your investments
  - Ignoring the news and sticking to your guns
  - Using an elegant approach to investment called '100 minus your age'
- looked at some simple options for your 'aggressive' and 'defensive' investments.

Arguably the single most important thing for any younger adult starting out on their journey here is to 'buy a big global equity index each month and chill', across your pension and investment accounts.

You should also ensure you have a decent amount of cash saved up and you might consider a bit of gold too, as we've seen. This combination of things is pretty simple and will get you a long way towards the result you need, certainly if you're under the age of 30.

If you start on this journey, it will also significantly increase the chance that you get interested in money and finance, particularly as you see your money grow.

If that happens for you, as you get older and hopefully have more to invest, you can then begin to make things a little more complicated, but only if you want to! As you head into your thirties and beyond, you might consider a wider range of 'aggressive' investments, and learn more about other 'defensive' options such as bond funds or property investments perhaps.

You might do this, or you might decide to just continue to keep things very simple and own a big global equity market. Many very wealthy people take precisely this approach and avoid overcomplicating things. After all, it is possible to put literally millions to work in a big equity ETF; many rich people do.

More generally, if you remember the magic of compounding, you will hopefully see that if you pay as much money into your investment accounts as possible and leave that money there for as long as possible, you will achieve the biggest result in terms of building your money. The more money you invest and the more you leave invested, the more 'free' money you can generate from compounding (interest on your interest, or return on your returns).

You will have to make your own decisions about when and for what reasons you withdraw money from your investment accounts, but the longer you leave it before upgrading your car or taking that holiday, the more cars and holidays you will be able to buy in the not-too-distant future, the more comfortable your retirement will be in the long run and the more free you are likely to be to leave a job you don't like.

As my economics teacher said to me in my first-ever lesson, economics is essentially all about:

Jam today or more jam tomorrow.

If you follow the logic outlined in this section of the book, you will very likely have done an extremely good job of setting up your finances, particularly for someone who doesn't want to invest a huge amount of time and effort in such things.

It shouldn't be too many years before you see a significant impact on your wealth. Your money will start making you money. If you stick with the plan for long enough, your money will very possibly end up making you more than you can earn by working – the ultimate goal of investment as we have seen throughout the book.

It is important to understand that there will very likely be years where you go backwards and lose money, but if you stick with it over long periods of time and buy regularly each month you should be fine in the long run.

It is very important to keep going. As I said earlier in the book, one of the biggest mistakes people make is to give up after only a few years or, even worse, after a few weeks or months! Investing is something you should do as an iron-clad commitment to yourself, as soon as you can and essentially for the whole of your working life. Thinking about it like that will maximize the chance that you get the life-changing result you deserve.

Conclusion

'Tell 'em what you're going to tell 'em. Tell 'em.
Tell 'em what you told 'em.'

– Paul White, first director of CBS News,
paraphrasing Dale Carnegie

The quote given above is well-known advice when you're making a presentation. It's also a useful idea in a book like this one because if you want to get a real-life outcome, all the ideas need to 'stick' and you need to take some action too!

If you have made it this far, my sincere congratulations. It is probably not an exaggeration to say that your financial knowledge is now better than that of a large proportion of the population – even including many finance professionals, economists and politicians (probably most politicians!).

I hope that you feel that you have learned enough to make a real and lasting difference to your financial affairs and, by extension, to your entire life.

In keeping with Paul White's quote above, I thought it might be useful to summarize what you have learned. Hopefully, as you finish the book, you are now up to speed on the following crucial points:

- Money isn't evil. It is just a technology – and arguably one of the most important we've ever invented as a species. It's critical for human flourishing, happiness and progress.
- You can and should be a saver and an investor.
- You must understand what is happening in the world today, particularly the pension situation we all face – the government can't pay for you!
- Even despite this, if you get investment right throughout your life, you should be fine!

- You *can* find the money for investment with a bit of thought and planning, particularly when it comes to your decisions about property.
- You need to learn about and benefit from the incredible power of compound interest.
- Today's financial accounts, products and sources of information are the best they've ever been.
- Investment works because of human progress – the most important investment theme of them all.
- There is high real inflation in the world – another reason that you must be an investor.
- You can keep things simple to begin with and learn more over time as you amass more money.

Another point to repeat as you end the book is that younger people have a huge advantage. People who learn about and start to invest in their twenties have a much higher probability of becoming wealthy than the majority of the population, who don't even think about such things until they're much older.

Another final thing to say is please spread the word. One of my all-time favourite quotes came from former US President John F. Kennedy, when he said:

> Ask not what your country can do for you – ask what you can do for your country.

All over the world, if we want our societies to flourish, we need many millions more people to take ownership of their finances, particularly given the points we've made about aging populations and how few countries can afford to provide their citizens with enough to live on for many decades of retirement. One of the most obvious solutions to this huge problem is for many more people to learn about investment. As you reach the end of this book, I would ask you to be part of that movement! Tell your friends and share the ideas in this book. Every single person who gets this sorted is a big win – for all of us!

I hope you have enjoyed the book and that you feel excited and empowered about what is possible with your money as a result.

I thank you for taking the time to read this far, and I wish you the very best for your future. If you are able to take control of your financial affairs, I have every confidence that it will yield wonderful results for every area of your life.

Happy investing!

Andrew Craig

Suggested reading

Botsman, Rachel, and Roo Rogers. *What's Mine is Yours: The Rise of Collaborative Consumption*. New York: Harper Business, 2010.

Clason, George S. *The Richest Man in Babylon – The Original 1926 Classic.* Reader's Library Classics, 2023.

Dalio, Ray. *Principles for Dealing with the Changing World Order: Why Nations Succeed or Fail*. Simon & Schuster, 2021.

Diamandis, Peter, and Steven Kotler. *Abundance: The Future is Better Than You Think*. Free Press, 2014.

Ferguson, Niall. *The Ascent of Money: A Financial History of the World*. Penguin, 2019.

Frisby, Dominic. *Bitcoin: The Future of Money?* Unbound, 2014.

Getty, J. Paul. *How to be Rich*. Jove Books, 1983.

Green, Alexander. *The Gone Fishin' Portfolio: Get Wise, Get Wealthy – and Get On with Your Life*. John Wiley & Sons, 2010.

Housel, Morgan. *The Psychology of Money: Timeless Lessons on Wealth, Greed, and Happiness.* Harriman House, 2020.

Kelly, Kevin. *The Inevitable: Understanding the 12 Technological Forces That Will Shape Our Future,* rep. edn. Penguin, 2017.

Kiyosaki, Robert T. *Rich Dad, Poor Dad: What the Rich Teach Their Kids about Money That the Poor and Middle Class Do Not!* Warner Business, 2000.

Lewis, Michael. *The Big Short: Inside the Doomsday Machine.* W. W. Norton & Company, 2010.

———. *Flash Boys: A Wall Street Revolt*. Penguin, 2015.

McWilliams, David. *Money: A Story of Humanity.* Simon & Schuster UK, 2024.

Olson, Jeff. *The Slight Edge,* 3rd rev. edn. Gazelle, 2013.

Parker, Christopher. *Harriman's New Book of Investing Rules: The Do's and Don'ts of the World's Best Investors.* Harriman House, 2017.

Rickards, James. *The New Case for Gold*. Portfolio, 2016.

Rosling, Hans, and Ola Rosling. *Factfulness: Ten Reasons We're Wrong about the World – And Why Things are Better Than You Think*. London: Sceptre, 2018.

Sethi, Ramit. *I Will Teach You to be Rich: No Guilt, No Excuses – Just a 6-Week Programme That Works.* Yellow Kite, 2020.

Shipman, Mark. *Big Money, Little Effort a Winning Strategy for Profitable Long-Term Investment*. Kogan Page Publishers, 2008.

———. *EQ vs IQ: The Reason Why Not Every Intelligent Trader or Investor is Rich*. CreateSpace, 2014.

Stanley, Thomas J., and William D. Danko. *The Millionaire Next Door: The Surprising Secrets of America's Wealthy.* Longstreet, 1996.

Image credits

Image on p. 108 Falkenstein/Bildagentur-online Historical Collect © Alamy
Image on p. 114 Anton_Ivanov © Shutterstock

Index

Page numbers followed by 'n' refer to footnotes.

RAISING READERS

Books Build Bright Futures

Dear Reader,

We'd love your attention for one more page to tell you about the crisis in children's reading, and what we can all do.

Studies have shown that reading for fun is the **single biggest predictor of a child's future life chances** – more than family circumstance, parents' educational background or income. It improves academic results, mental health, wealth, communication skills, ambition and happiness.[1]

The number of children reading for fun is in rapid decline. Young people have a lot of competition for their time. In 2024, 1 in 10 children and young people in the UK aged 5 to 18 did not own a single book at home.[2]

Hachette works extensively with schools, libraries and literacy charities, but here are some ways we can all raise more readers:

- Reading to children for just 10 minutes a day makes a difference
- Don't give up if children aren't regular readers – there will be books for them!
- Visit bookshops and libraries to get recommendations
- Encourage them to listen to audiobooks
- Support school libraries
- Give books as gifts

There's a lot more information about how to encourage children to read on our website: **www.RaisingReaders.co.uk**

Thank you for reading.

hachette UK

[1] OECD, '21st-Century Readers: Developing Literacy Skills in a Digital World', 2021, https://www.oecd.org/en/publications/21st-century-readers_a83d84cb-en.html

[2] National Literacy Trust, 'Book Ownership in 2024', November 2024, https://literacytrust.org.uk/research-services/research-reports/book-ownership-in-2024